# Mozar
# & M

## The Insiders' Guide to a Short Break in Salzburg, Berchtesgaden and the Bavarian Alps
## By
## Yvonne Salisbury

# Copyright

Copyright © 2009 by Yvonne Salisbury.
All Photos © 2009 by Yvonne Salisbury.
First Published 2009
Last Updated September 2017

All rights reserved. No part of this publication may be reproduced in any form without the written consent of the copyright owner.
The author has done her best to ensure the accuracy and completeness of this guide, all prices and information correct at the time of publication. However, she can accept no responsibility for any loss, injury, or inconvenience sustained as a result of information or advice in this guide.

*"You're not here for a long time, just a good time"*

Printed and distributed by **Insiders' Guides**

For all guides in the Insiders Guides Series see
www.insidersguide-online.com

## Preface

Salzburg is a compact city and most of Salzburg's main attractions are conveniently located near the old town. It is the old town that has the most charm with narrow streets that lead to cobbled squares. With castles, churches, markets and a variety of shops there is plenty to see and do in Salzburg. It is a beautiful city, famous for Mozart and The Sound of Music and declared a World Heritage Site by UNESCO in 1997.

Berchtesgaden has attracted tourists since the Royal Family began bringing visitors here in the early 1800's. Visitors over the centuries have included German Emperors, the French king Napoleon III, the Kings of

Egypt and Belgium and more recently Prince Rainier and Princess Grace of Monaco. Today however, tourists flock here for the vast array of year round sorts, the continual beauty of the National Park and the history of the Obersalzberg. Despite tourist numbers increasing, the area is unspoilt and retains the rural charm it has always had.

*"The Berchtesgaden area is a jewel of nature"*
Crown Princess Marie Gabriele of Bavaria, 1878 – 1912.

These 2 areas are situated only 15 miles from each other so can be visited as day trips from either destination or are ideal for a 2 centre holiday, city and mountains.

## **Contents**

Salzburg
Things to See and Do
Market Squares
Sound of Music
Shopping
Sports
Seasonal Events
Christmas Markets
Food and Drink
Sleep
Berchtesgaden
History
Berchtesgaden and The Bavarian Royal Family
Berchtesgaden and The Third Reich
Towns and Lakes
National Park
Things to See and Do
Food and Drink
German Alpine Road
sleep
Getting to Salzburg and Berchtesgaden
Planes, Trains and Automobiles
Useful Information
About the Author

# **Salzburg**

Think of Salzburg and most people think of Mozart or The Sound of Music, but this compact city has so much more to offer visitors. Situated at the edge of the Alps, just over the border from Bavaria, less than 2 hours' drive from Munich and 150 miles from the Austrian capital of Vienna. Straddling both banks of the Salzach River, the car-free cobbled streets lead to medieval stone houses and Italianate marble palaces, wood-panelled taverns and numerous galleries and museums. There are five bridges that connect the two sides of the river, the Nonntal Bridge and State Bridge, and 3 pedestrian bridges; Mozart Footbridge, Makart Footbridge and Mülln Footbridge.

The left bank of the Salzach is the Altstadt or "older part" where ancient Roman settlements once stood. The right bank is the more modern part of the city but can still boast buildings over a century old and has played its part in history.

The salt trade gave Salzburg its name and wealth, but Archbishop Wolf Dietrich von Raitenau is responsible for the grandeur and architecture. He commissioned Italian architects to design the grand cathedral, five squares and the Mirabell Palace.

The Hohensalzburg fortress sits high above the city. For centuries, it repelled attackers; today you arrive via the funicular railway, keen to see the striking panoramic views of the city that can be viewed from the walls.

Salzburg's place in the spotlight was guaranteed when Wolfgang Amadeus

Mozart was born there in 1756. Although the Mozart name is attached to everything, from the airport to cafés, his is not the only music in town. This city stages some 4,200 concerts a year, morning, noon and night. From the world renowned summer festival to the informality of the autumn jazz festival, Salzburg loves all sorts of music.

On the outskirts of the city, there is the Hellbrunn Palace. Some visitors are drawn for the Renaissance gardens, others for the schoolboy humour provided by hidden spouts in the water garden. The Sound of Music fans photograph the gazebo where Liesl met Franz, and, during Advent, everyone enjoys one of Austria's prettiest Christmas markets.

## Weather

The weather in Salzburg during the winter can be very cold due to its alpine location and the city often experiences snowfall. Summer temperatures average in the mid 20's but again due to the city's proximity to the mountains showers can be frequent, but that should not deter you from visiting this beautiful city.

## History

Salzburg can be regarded as the oldest and most important cultural and spiritual centre in present day Austria. A settlement here can be traced back as far as Neolithic times but Salzburg's history really begins when it was the seat of the Archbishopric of Salzburg during the Holy Roman Empire. It was elevated to the rank of archdiocese in 798 and from the late Middle Ages onwards had formed a spiritual principality in the Holy Roman Empire.

The city has changed hands many times between Austria and Bavaria. The development of the region and its ultimate separation from Bavaria was agreed in the fourteenth century. In 1805 the city was annexed to the Austrian Empire, returning to Bavarian rule in 1809 and back to Austria once more in 1815. Of Austria's present day lands, Salzburg is the only one to have been ruled, as an independent state by a prince-archbishop and it is the only one of the many spiritual principalities of the Holy Roman Empire still to exist as an independent land.

# Things to See and Do

Most of Salzburg's main attractions are conveniently located near the old town and therefore all within easy walking distance. It is the old town that has the most charm with narrow streets that lead to cobbled squares. With castles, churches, markets and a variety of shops there is plenty to see and do in Salzburg.

**The Top 10 Things to See and do in Salzburg:**

Hohensalzburg Fortress
Mozart's Birthplace
Mozart's Residence
Salzburg Cathedral
Hellbrunn Palace and Fountains
Salzburg Museum
Museum of Modern Art Mönchsberg
Museum of Natural History
Residence Gallery
Salzburg Zoo

**Top Tip:**
**The Salzburg Card**

Salzburg Card is your key to sightseeing in the city of Salzburg: it provides free admission to many of Salzburg's museums, free use of the Fortress funicular, free public transport, Mozart's birthplace and much more. Salzburg Card holders can also receive discounts on concerts, theatre performances or excursions to other destinations in the Salzburg area.

The card is available to buy in 24, 48 and 72 hour length time frames and prices are from 12 euros a child and 24 euros per adult.

The Salzburg Card is available at most hotel reception desks, at all of the tourist information offices and at ticket offices or can be bought online before you arrive. Current prices are available in the Salzburg Card brochure. All services used are automatically deducted from your card.

# Hohensalzburg Fortress

Jan – April, Oct – Dec 9.30am – 5pm; May – Sept 9am to 7pm
Free entry with Salzburg Card
www.hohensalzburgcastle.com

The Hohensalzburg Fortress is a monument of over 900 years history and is one of the largest existing 11th century fortresses in Europe.

Built in 1077 by Archbishop Gebhart, the fortress has dominated the city from top of the Mönchsberg and despite many attempts has never been invaded. As a faithful servant of the Pope, Archbishop Gebhart von Salzburg held the strongholds of Hohensalzburg, Hohenwerfen and Friesach. The four main towers along the outer wall named the "Glockenturm", the "Trompeterturm", the "Krautturm" and the "Schmiedturm" or "Arrestantenturm" were built by Prince Archbishop Burkhard III von Weißpriach in the mid-15th century. From Festungsgasse the fortress can be reached by a funicular railway, first introduced in 1515 and still working today, albeit in a modernized form.

During the 15th and 16th centuries, Salzburg was involved in the turmoil of the so-called Hungarian War and the Peasants' War, and the archbishops took refuge behind the battlements of the fortress. It was during this period that the main building was enlarged and the arsenal and the granary built. The fortress' interior was richly decorated: intricate Gothic woodcarvings and ornamental paintings adorn the Golden Hall and the Golden Chamber. One of the last extensive modifications was the addition of the great Kuenberg bastion.

Having served as a fortification and temporary residence of the prince archbishops for many years, the fortress also served as military barracks and a prison. Prince Archbishop Wolf Dietrich was held captive in the fortress by his nephew and successor, Markus Sittikus, from 1612 until his death in 1617.

Today the fortress is open to the public all year round; besides the medieval rooms the romantic courtyard and the bastions regularly serve as scenery for events such as the Fortress Concerts, special dinner evenings and a small Christmas market in December.

## Mozart

Wolfgang Amadeus Mozart was born in Salzburg in 1756. His father was a musician in the Royal Court. In 1762 the family went on tour to the royal courts of Vienna and Munich and this was followed the next year by tours to Germany, Belgium, France and London.

## Mozart's Birthplace

Getreidegasse 9
9am to 5.30pm daily
www.mozarteum.at
Free entry with Salzburg Card

The Mozart family lived on the third floor of the "Hagenauer House" at Getreidegasse 9 for twenty-six years, from 1747 to 1773. The building is named after the merchant and toy dealer, Johann Hagenauer, who owned the building and was a friend of the Mozart family. The celebrated composer was born here on January 27, 1756.

The International Mozarteum Foundation first installed a museum in Mozart's Birthplace in 1880, and it has been enlarged over the years and now attracts thousands of visitors every year. The displays include historic instruments, documents, memorabilia and most of the portraits painted during his lifetime, including the unfinished oil painting "Mozart at the

Piano" painted by Mozart's brother-in-law, Joseph Lange, in 1789. The famous exhibits include Mozart's childhood violin, his concert violin, his clavichord, the harpsichord, portraits and letters from the Mozart family.

## Mozart's Residence

Makartplatz 8
9am to 5.30pm daily (8pm July and August)
Free entry with Salzburg Card

In 1773 it became apparent to Mozart's father that the house on Getreidegasse was too small for the family and they moved into a more spacious house across the river on Makartplatz. Here Mozart composed much of his music and symphonies. In his capacity as the court organist and concert-master, Wolfgang Amadeus Mozart composed numerous works of sacred music for Salzburg. Mozart's father lived alone in the house after being widowed in 1784 until his death in 1787. The building was badly damaged by a bomb in 1944 and later purchased by the Mozarteum Foundation in 1989.

# Salzburger Dom (Salzburg Cathedral)

January, February, November:
Monday-Saturday 8am - 5pm, Sunday & holiday 1pm - 5pm
March, April, October, December:
Monday-Saturday 8am - 6pm, Sunday & holiday 1pm - 6pm
May, June, July, and September:
Monday-Saturday 8am - 7pm, Sunday & holiday 1pm - 7pm
August:
Monday-Saturday 8am - 8pm, Sunday & holiday 1pm - 8pm
No visits during Mass

www.salzburger-dom.at

Salzburg's Cathedral is probably the city's most significant piece of sacred architecture, with its magnificent façade, mighty dome and two towers it dominates the city skyline. Destroyed by fire and rebuilt, enlarged and expanded, it bears witness to the power and independence of Salzburg's archbishops, each seeming to want to out-do his predecessor.

Bishop Virgil, who came to Salzburg in 767, built the first cathedral on this site and in 774 the cathedral was consecrated to St. Virgil and St. Rupert. The city was set on fire in 1167, and as well as many other buildings, the cathedral was destroyed. Rebuilt ten years later under the rule of Archbishop Conrad III of Wittelsbach, the cathedral became more beautiful, magnificent and impressive than ever, making it the mightiest Romanesque cathedral north of the Alps.

Four hundred years later another fire raged and destroyed large sections of the cathedral in December 1598. This enabled Archbishop Wolf Dietrich the opportunity to tear down the damaged cathedral and to make plans for its reconstruction. The Salzburg residents were outraged at the archbishop's ruthless plans; not only were valuable sculptures and gravestones of the archbishops destroyed but the cathedral cemetery turned over and the bones of the dead piled on the debris. His quarrel with Bavaria over salt mining rights led to his arrest and imprisonment in the Hohensalzburg Fortress by his nephew Markus Sittikus, and this put an end to the various construction plans of Wolf Dietrich. After Wolf Dietrich's death, Archbishop Markus Sittikus made plans to rebuild the Cathedral, which became the first early Baroque church north of the Alps, although he did not live to see the consecration of the Cathedral by

Archbishop Paris in 1628. The towers were completed in 1652 and 1655.

In 1944 the dome and part of the chancel were destroyed during a bomb attack. The necessary renovations were carried out to return the Cathedral to its former glory and it was reconsecrated in 1959. Today, the cathedral can seat around 900 worshippers.

The three dates found in the gates to the Cathedral are in memory of the three consecrations: "774, 1628 and 1959". Four statues are located in front of the main façade: the apostles Peter and Paul with keys and sword as well as the two patron saints Rupert and Virgil with a salt box and a model of the church. Behind the four statues you find the main entrance to the Cathedral. The three bronze gates were added in 1957 and 1958 and represent the three divine virtues; the Gate of Faith on the left, the central Gate of Love and the Gate of Hope on the right.

Among the precious objects to be found in the Cathedral is the baptismal font in which Mozart was baptised, the beautiful main organ surrounded by angels playing instruments and crowned by Rupert and Virgil, as well as the magnificent Cathedral portals. The bells in the tower are named Barbara, Leonhard, Virgil, Johannes, Maria, Rupertus and Salvator.

## Hellbrunn Palace

Fürstenweg 37
9am – 5.30 pm April to October
www.hellbrunn.at
Free entry with Salzburg Card

Located just to the south of the city, this palace was built in 1612 by Archbishop Markus Sittikus, shortly after he came to the throne, in the Italian Renaissance style that he admired so much. He wanted a summer residence "villa suburbana" with space and elegance. The palace was primarily used as the site of luxurious celebrations and festivities, spectacular events and cultural highlights. The magnificent ballrooms are still used today.

The gardens are well worth a visit, see the water theme that is continuous through the gardens, trickling through trees and bushes, and the "trick" fountains that are world famous. For romantic evenings you can take guided tours in the evening throughout July and August and enjoy an evening of water, light and music.

The grounds are a beautiful, peaceful place for a walk or perhaps for the children to enjoy the adventure playground. The natural stone quarry in Hellbrunn was transformed into a stage, creating the "Steintheater" (Stone Theatre), the oldest open-air stage in Europe.

The pavilion from "The Sound of Music" is now located here.

## Salzburg Museum

Mozartplatz 1
Tues – Sun 9am – 5pm, also Monday 9am to 5pm in July, August and December
www.salzburgmuseum.at

The Salzburg Museum, a winner of the Austrian Museum prize, has been recently refurbished and houses fine displays of architecture, science, art and archaeology. The museum's new concept combines valuable objects of art, artistic presentations, interesting facts and multimedia installations into a harmonious exhibition.

On the first floor the "Salzburg – up close" is a display that tells the story of Salzburg over the centuries and the men and women who have played their part in developing the city. The second floor houses "Salzburg – The Myth" and shows the development of art, history and culture in the city through the ages. The Mirror Hall displays archaeology and medieval collections and takes visitors on a journey into the distant past. The inner courtyard or "Art Hall" shows three main collections a year and lies beneath the inner courtyard of the Neue Residenz. The Panorama Passage is a walkway connecting the Salzburg Museum with the Panorama Museum. Along the passage you can view archaeological excavation, models of the city and historical data about the development of Salzburg. The Salzburg Museum is proof that a modern museum can inform and yet at the same time entertain its visitors.

## Museum of Modern Art

Mönchsberg 32 and
Wiener-Philharmoniker-Gasse 9
www.museumdermoderne.at

Free entry with Salzburg Card

The Museum der Moderne Salzburg houses collections at two different locations in the city: the Rupertinum in the historic city centre, a baroque building for new artistic concepts and the other at the Mönchsberg, looking over the rooftops of the old city, shows modern art in a contemporary setting. Together, the buildings offer over 3,000 cubic metres of exhibition space for themed modern art exhibitions from the 20th and 21st centuries, with over 17,000 works of Austrian photographic art on display.

The Baroque building of the Rupertinum was given to the city of Salzburg in 1983 in order to house a modern art museum and in particular graphic and photographic art in the constantly changing exhibitions.

The Mönchsberg museum opened on the edge of the steep Mönchsberg cliff in 2004; the outer façade is covered with local Untersberg marble.

## Museum of Natural History

Museumsplatz 5
9am to 5pm daily
www.hausdernatur.at
Free entry with Salzburg Card

The Museum of Natural History in Salzburg is one of the biggest attractions for visitors and has an aquarium, reptile zoo, dinosaur hall, world of crystal, space show, journey through the human body, the Salzach lifeline, sea world and science centre.

The Aquarium is considered to be one of the most beautiful aquariums in Central Europe, and is a particularly popular attraction for young and old. Its 36 tanks present the wonders of underwater life. The colourful tropical fish and close-up observation of the inhabitants of the Mediterranean, the Amazon or local waters is a fascinating experience.

Living reptiles and amphibians can be found in the Reptile Zoo, where approximately 200 animals inhabit 56 terrariums. As well as domestic snakes there are well-known poisonous snakes from all over the world as well as water and land turtles, lizards, frogs and alligators.

The Space Research Hall features an original size display of the moon landing, a space station of the future, a mercury spacecraft in original size as well as a number of model rockets.

The Science Centre offers visitors a variety of exciting new experiences: technology, natural science and the human body all become an interactive adventure. There are 80 hands on stations that allow visitors to operate turbines or hear and feel the music in a walk-in violin. Hands-on fun and excitement are guaranteed for all the family.

Other exhibits include minerals, geology, European mammals, birds, and the animal habitats of the Ice Age, America, Africa, Australia and Asia and last but not least an exhibit dedicated to man and his domestic animals. There are continuously changing special exhibits to complete the extensive program.

An outdoor café provides the necessary refreshments between the different exhibitions.

**Residence and Gallery**

Residenzplatz 1
Tuesday to Sunday, 10am to 5pm
www.residenzgalerie.at

For centuries the prince bishops used the Salzburg Residenz as a magnificent place to live. Visitors requesting an audience with the bishops were exposed to demonstrations of power and authority as only the most important individuals allowed into the most magnificent rooms.

The Residenz was used over the centuries as a place to entertain important guests and continues to do so today. In 1867 Emperor Franz Josef and his wife Elisabeth entertained Napoleon here. More recently prominent political leaders and crowned heads of State have been welcomed here.

Today the Residenz is one of the most impressive attractions in Salzburg, an extensive complex of buildings with over 180 rooms and three courtyards. An audio guide tour of the state rooms on the 2nd floor of the Residenz palace is offered in 8 languages and takes about 45 minutes.

The tour includes the most beautiful rooms, here are just some of the highlights:

The Carabinieri Saal was used as a common room for the bodyguards of the prince bishops and has precious ceiling frescos, as well as floors made of Adnet marble.
The Ratszimmer (Councillors Room) is where Mozart first performed at court at the age of 6. The Rittersaal was, and still is, often used for concerts due to its excellent acoustics and as his father was orchestra director the young Mozart also played here too. Other rooms of note include the Throne Room and the Emperor's Hall also known as the Emperor's Chamber with portraits of Habsburg Emperors and Kings.

The magnificent atmosphere of the Residence Gallery is the ideal location for Salzburg's state collection and reflects the character of the city. The Residence Gallery houses not only the State of Salzburg's art collection but also European paintings from the 16th to 19th century. The collections focus on Dutch, and Italian, French paintings from the 17th and 18th centuries and Austrian paintings from the last 400 years.

In addition to its own changing exhibitions, there are regular special visiting exhibitions, providing an interesting contrast between historic and contemporary art.

It is recommended you check the website or tourist office as the Gallery is closed on various dates throughout the year.

**Top Tip:**
A combi ticket for individual visitors entitles the holder to admission to the Residenz and also the gallery on the 3rd floor of the building.

### Carillon (Glockenspiel)

The famous Salzburg Glockenspiel crowns the bell tower of the Residence on the western side. The 35 bells were cast in Antwerp between 1688 and 1689 and the mechanism and brass drum manufactured in 1702 by Salzburg gunsmith Franz Sulzer, and the bell founder, Benedikt Eisenberger. In 1873, watchmaker Johann Baptist Fischer installed a special system that triggered the playing mechanism and there are 7,964 holes drilled in the drum required to operate the chimes.

The carillon has operated in Salzburg since 1704 and has recently undergone substantial restoration and maintenance. It currently plays approximately 40 tunes, of which 16 are attributed to Johann Michael Haydn. The pieces by Mozart and his father are adaptations from the 19th century.

Guided tours are conducted from the end of March to the end of October usually on Thursdays at 5:30 am and Fridays at 10:30 am.

The Glockenspiel plays at 7:00am, 11:00am and 6:00pm daily.

**Salzburg Zoo**

Anifer Landesstrasse 1
Anif
www.zoo.salzburg.at
9am - 4pm winter
9am – 5pm spring & autumn
9am – 6pm summer
Free entry with Salzburg Card

A visit to the zoo is always a favourite attraction with families and this one is no exception. With over 800 animals from over 140 species there is plenty to see and do. One of the main aims of Salzburg's zoo is keeping animals, both native and exotic, in an environment close to their natural habitat. The zoo aims to ensure balance and harmony between the beauty of the local landscape in Hellbrunn and the natural environment of the animals. These factors make your visit a more attractive and enjoyable experience.

## Leopoldskron Palace

Leopoldskronstrasse 56 - 58
www.schloss-leopoldskron.com

This rococo palace was built in 1731 adjacent to an existing lake, and just a short walk from the old town. It changed hands many times in the nineteenth century and eventually in 1918 came under the ownership of Max Reinhardt, founding director of the Salzburg Festival. The façade was used in "the Sound of Music" as was the lake, the pavilion was originally located on the far side of the lake until it was moved to Hellbrunn. Today the Palace is not open to the public but the organised Sound of Music tours do include it on the itinerary. Today it is used for seminars and weddings.

## Mirabell Palace & Gardens

Mirabellplatz
Palace: Monday, Wednesday, Thursday 8am to 4pm; Tuesday and Friday 1pm to 4pm Closed for official occasions
Gardens 6am to dusk daily
Free Entry

Situated just across the river in the newer part of the city the Mirabell Palace was built in 1606 by Prince Archbishop Wolf Dietrich for his love Salome Alt.

The Marble Hall has always been used a banqueting hall and today is considered to be one of the most romantic wedding settings anywhere.

The famous gardens are laid out in a geometric pattern, with four groups of statues around the Grand Fountain symbolising the four elements; fire, water, air and earth. The Hedge Theatre, created between 1704 and 1718, is located in the main part of the Mirabell Gardens and is one of the oldest hedge theatres north of the Alps. Emperor Franz Joseph opened the Mirabell Gardens to the public in 1854. The Pegasus Fountain was installed in 1913. The Dwarf Garden was created during the rule of Archbishop Franz Anton Furst Harrach and consisted of 28 dwarves carved from the white marble of the Untersberg. The gardens are also the location of the famous steps that were used by Maria to teach the children to sing in the Sound of Music. Today the gardens are a horticultural masterpiece and popular backdrop for photographers.

Today the palace houses the offices of the Mayor of Salzburg.

**Petersfriedhof (St Peters Cemetery)**

6.30 am to 7pm summer; 6.30am to 5pm winter

This is one of the oldest cemeteries in Salzburg and considered to be one of the most beautiful in the world. You can enter after leaving the funicular railway down from Hohensalzburg by turning immediately to your left. The cemetery nestles up against the stone of the hill and you can visit the catacombs that date from the year 700. There are many elaborate gravestones to be seen and the sisters of both Haydn and Mozart are buried here.

## Stift Nonnberg

Nonnberggasse 2
7am to dusk (except during Mass)

The convent can be reached on foot over the Hoher Weg, from the Kaigasse over the steps of the Nonnbergstiege and from Nonntal through a narrow lane. The convent and the museum are not open to the public, however it is possible to visit the church. The church is built in Gothic style and the twelfth century frescoes are world famous and of very high quality.

## Salzburg Heimatwerk

Residenzplatz 9
9am to 6pm Monday to Friday, 9am to 5pm Saturday

Situated beneath the Glockenspiel and the Neue Residence, the Salzburg Folk Heritage Society ("Salzburger Heimatwerk") first opened its doors to visitors in 1946. The aim is to promote the region's folk culture, by organising cultural events and commercial enterprise. This includes the preservation and on-going development of traditions handed down through the generations, particularly with regard to handicrafts, folk costume, traditions, music, and song and dance. This is a great place to buy souvenirs whilst supporting traditional local crafts.

Created in the workshops at the hands of master craftsmen are the unique, custom–made folk costumes, which reflect both traditional and modern times. Beautiful block prints, fine hand-woven fabrics, silks, colourful prints and exquisite table linens can also be purchased at the Heimatwerk, as can the original Salzburg bells that are so highly sought-after by collectors. There is a huge selection of food gifts including jams and chutneys, honey, vinegars, pesto and oils and to name just a few.

The Salzburger Heimatwerk is also the organizer of the "Salzburg Advent Singing" on the cathedral steps, one of the most enjoyable cultural events in the entire Alpine region. Special exhibitions, changing from season to season, are also well worth a visit.

## Hellbrunner Allee

The Hellbrunner Allee connects the Residenz and the old town of Salzburg with Hellbrunn Castle in the south, a distance of about 5 kilometres. Prince Archbishop Markus Sittikus ordered the construction of the path so he could easily get to Hellbrunn Palace from the city.

Today, most of the Hellbrunner Allee remains open and the mighty chestnut trees demonstrate there has been little change since the 17th century. Many locals walk their dogs in this area, and a number of villas show that this is one of Salzburg's most expensive areas.

Just keep walking southwards and you will without doubt recognise the characteristic yellow building, Schloss Frohnburg. Originally built between 1660 and 1680 by Prince Archbishop Max Gandolf as a summer residence, today it is among the many attractions worshipped by thousands of fans of the movie "The Sound of Music", in which it was used for the exterior shots of the Trapp residence. Today Schloss Frohnburg is owned by Salzburger Universität Mozarteum, the art University, and serves as a dormitory and concert venue.

## Salzburger Freilicht Museum
www.freilichtmuseum.com

April – October Tuesday to Sunday 9am – 6pm
July and August Daily 9am to 6pm

This open air museum is located just 10 kilometres from Salzburg in the Untersberg Nature Park. There are over 100 historic buildings, from 6 centuries displaying agriculture, crafts and industry. Visitors can take a tour of the museum on the train and see farms, the village school, brewery, mills, tractors, steam engines and much more.

There is a traditional restaurant for snacks and a large playground for children. There are several special events throughout the year including Easter egg hunts, special exhibitions, folk dancing and handicrafts every Sunday.

# Market Squares

There are numerous market squares in Salzburg for you to walk round and look at.

## Alter Markt

The Old Marketplace was laid out in the thirteenth century. The market sold goods such as dairy, herbs and vegetables here until the mid-nineteenth century when it moved to University square. It is lined with the burghers houses that can trace their origin back to Middle Ages, although today's shops representing more modern architecture surround the market. The smallest house in Salzburg is only 1.4 metres wide and can be seen next to Tomaselli coffee house. You still see some market stalls here today selling dried flowers and such like.

## Domplatz

Reached by passing under an arch from Residenzplatz, the main feature of this square in front of the Cathedral is the Immaculate Column. The column and statue of the Virgin Mary are similar to the ones in Munich and Vienna and was designed by brothers Wolfgang and Johann Baptist Hagenauer. It is surrounded by 4 figures; Angel, Devil, Truth and the Church and their meaning are explained on a plaque to the side. Today the square is used during the festival in the summer months and a market at

Christmas.

## Hagenauerplatz

Although probably one of the most visited squares in Salzburg, the majority of visitors are unlikely to realize they have visited this square. It is where you stand to look at the façade of Mozart's birthplace, which is located at the top of the square on Getreidegasse. In the sixteenth century the fish market was held here.

## Mozartplatz

Situated just at the end of Getreidegasse, Mozartplatz was originally called Michaelsplatz. The name of the square was changed in 1842 when his 2 sons unveiled the statue to Mozart. The Bavarian King, Ludwig I, was a great contributor to the monument as Mozart had often performed at his Royal Court. The unveiling of the statue was delayed by a year, as an important Roman mosaic was uncovered during the sighting of the monument.

## Residenzplatz

This is one of the largest squares in Salzburg and is nestled between Mozartplatz and Domplatz. The square is surrounded by the New Residence, the Old Residence, the Cathedral and a continuous row of buildings that were once houses but are now shops. The central fountain is considered to be one of the most beautiful in the city and was commissioned by Archbishop Thun, a fountain enthusiast. The fountain features horses, giants, dolphins and a triton and is well worth a closer look.

Today the square is used for sports or musical concerts and New Year's Eve parties. St Rupert's Fair is held here in September as well as the Christmas market in December.
Horse and carriage rides leave from Residenzplatz and take tours of the city.

## Makartplatz

Named after the painter, Hans Makart, this square is opposite the Mirabell Gardens. The square is dominated by the baroque styled Church of the

Holy Trinity, the most significant sacred building on the right bank of the city and it was at number 8 Makartplatz that the Mozart family lived. From Makartplatz you can enter the Mirabell Gardens.

**Karajan Square**

Herbert von Karajan Square is located against the face of the Mönchsberg, at the far end of Getreidegasse, in front of Sigmund's Gate. Originally named after Archbishop Sigismund Christian Schrattenbach, the square was renamed in honour of the world famous conductor, Herbert von Karajan. Sigmund's Gate connects the Old City with the Riedenburg district and is the oldest road tunnel in Austria.

The Large Festival Hall, Old University and Hotel Goldener Hirsch are close to the square.

The magnificent Horse Pond was designed and built in 1693 by Johann Bernhard Fischer von Erlach whilst building the facade for the royal stables. The central group, the "Horse Tamer" by Michael Bernhard Mandl, once stood in the royal stables. Archbishop Firmian restored the Horse Pond in 1732, when the statue of the "Horse Tamer" was rotated 90 degrees and placed on a new base and a balustrade was placed around the basin. Josef Ebner painted the horse frescoes on the rear wall.

# Sound of Music

Salzburg is of course famous for being the location for the film "The Sound of Music" which tells the story of the von Trapp family.

The film itself is based on a true story. Born in Vienna, Maria von Kutschera was living as a novice candidate at the Benedictine Convent on Nonnberg in Salzburg when she was sent by her Mother Superior as a governess to the household of Baron Georg von Trapp to look after his seven children, left motherless after the death of his wife. Shortly afterwards Maria became the Baron's wife and in the early 30's she founded a family choir with which she undertook frequent public performances whilst they remained in Austria.

After fleeing the country on Hitler's annexation of Austria in 1938, the family had no income other than that raised from their musical performances. Their success in the USA, however, proved sufficient to enable them to settle there and, in 1941, to purchase a farm in Stowe, Vermont, which ultimately became the Trapp Family Lodge, now a successful hotel. It was here that Maria wrote her memoirs in 1952 upon which the film is based.

Many of the locations can be visited; The Benedictine Convent at Nonnberg (Maria), the Mirabell Gardens (Do Re Mi), St Peters Cemetery, Leopoldskron Palace which was used as the façade, the Pavilion is today located at Hellbrunn Palace and the Residenz Square where Maria boards the bus. If you look carefully at the beginning of the film, as Maria crosses the Domplatz to board the bus, you can see the real Maria von Trapp walk past the arches.

There are many organised tours of the locations and these can be booked at the Tourist Office in Mozartplatz.

## **Shopping**

Shopping in the old town of Salzburg is an atmospheric experience, narrow beautiful streets, delicious smells from bakers and coffee shops and olde world charm. The narrow streets are filled small independent shops with their elaborate facades and wrought iron signs, along with well-known chains.

Getreidegasse is probably the best-known street in Salzburg. Tall buildings on each side add to the charm and many of the passages that link the streets have been converted to shops or mini arcades. At Christmas time the street is strung from side to side with small white lights which add to the atmosphere.

The shopping streets of the old town around Getreidegasse are largely a pedestrian zone with the exception of delivery vehicles and taxis. Goldgasse gets its name from the goldsmiths that once had their shops here. It is possible still today to buy jewellery new and old from the shops that nestle together in this narrow street that leads to Residenzplatz.

Whether it is designer fashions, traditional "Trachten" Austrian clothing, souvenirs or chocolates they can all be found in the 800 or so stores that pack this area. Some stores focus on just one product, for example there is a store that sells only hand painted eggs for all occasions - Christmas, Easter and Halloween to name a few.

Mozart souvenirs such as CD's, books, coins, music or postcards are very popular. If you are interested in a souvenir from the Salzburg Festival, CD's can be purchased from most souvenir or music stores. At Christmas time souvenirs featuring the carol "Silent Night" are popular gifts to take home.

You will find a good selection of chocolates to buy, including the famous Mozartkugeln, which are made from chocolate, marzipan and praline. Also on sale are bottles of Mozart chocolate liqueur in milk, plain or flavoured varieties.

One of the oldest stores in Salzburg is located in the Alter Markt. Steindl ladies wear has been here for 4 generations and prides itself in high quality clothing and high quality service. Even if you do not venture in it is worth looking at the beautiful clothes in the window, especially in winter when the windows display fabulous cloaks and coats.

There is also a Christmas shop that is open all year round near to the Mozartplatz. Here you can find all types of tree decorations on several floors.

Across the river in the newer part of town near to the Mirabell Gardens you will also find a selection of stores

Stores are open from 10am to 6pm Monday to Friday and 10am to 5pm on Saturdays. You may find some stores open outside these hours and some souvenir shops may be open on Sundays but other shops will be closed.

**Designer Outlet Salzburg**
Kasernenstraße
5073 Wals-Siezenheim

Opening Times: 09:30 – 19:00
Friday 09:30 – 21:00
Saturday 09:00 – 18:00
Closed Sunday
Designer Outlet Salzburg attracts visitors with the stylish elegance of its traditional Shopping arcades and a selection of stores and designers that is hard to beat. Fashion for women, men and children, shoes and accessories, watches and jewellery, sportswear, along with lifestyle accessories and exciting gift ideas. With over 200 top labels including famous names such as Michael Kors, Calvin Klein, Desigual, Diesel, Guess, Hugo Boss, Tom Tailor Denim, X-Bionic, Puma and Samsonite and all of this at prices reduced by 30 to 70 percent

## Traditional Specialist Stores

## Bakers

The **Stiftsbäckerei St Peter** is adjacent the St Peters Cemetery and is the oldest bakers in Salzburg, dating back as far as the twelfth century. The bakery, with its historic vaults, stands as a reminder of days long past. In its original wood-burning ovens, the beloved "wood-oven bread" is still baked from pure, natural sourdough. The bread keeps well and is just as good with butter and jam, as well as with ham and cheese.

The **Bäckerei Holztrattner** lies just off the Alter Markt in Brodgasse. The bakery is warm and inviting and enticing smells fill the air. On sale are a large assortment of breads, flatbreads and rolls alongside succulent Topfengolatschen pockets, delicious Danish pastries and traditional Kletzenbrot fruit bread. The owner, Eva Holztrattner, loves to travel to Italy in search of ideas for new specialties, and her wonderful Grissini and many other delicious treats testify to this.

# Confectioners

Cakes and exquisite confectionary are part of everyday life in Salzburg so make sure you take time to sit and enjoy the tradition of cake and coffee and take a few treats home. If you are counting calories, don't bother just relax and enjoy!

**Café Konditorei Fürst**, located in Brodgasse first opened in 1884. Fifteen years after he created the original, confectioner Paul Fürst, received a gold medal at the Paris Exhibition for his Salzburger Mozartkugel, which was already popular far beyond Austria's borders. He chose the name for his nougat-pistachio temptation to honour Salzburg's greatest son, who was at that time not as popular as he is today. Today, those "Original Salzburger Mozartkugeln" continue to be hand-made by the House of Fürst, using the same manufacturing process and the same recipe.

Apart from this sweet treat, great-grandson, Norbert Fürst, offers a broad selection of other chocolates and truffle specialties, along with mouthwatering pastries and classic coffee creations. There is another coffee house at Mirabellplatz 5, while visitors can also obtain their chocolates at Getreidegasse No. 47.

Master confectioner Heidi Ratzka runs **Konditorei Ratzka** on Imbergstrasse and she has successfully followed in her father's footsteps. Gourmet Wolfgang Siebeck personally crowned her father "Emperor of Confectioners", while Austria's gourmet guide, the Gault Millau, acclaimed this family run establishment as the country's very best confectioners.

As many as 20 different cakes are created each and every day in the tiny bakery and as you look in the display cases, you probably wish you could sample every single one of them; the apricot Marillenfleck, the Parisian Cream, cheese, poppy, rowanberry or almond Wachauer and tortes, to name but a few, as well as delicate petit fours and homemade cookies.

If you manage to grab one of the few seats available in this small confectioner you should count yourself lucky. To this day, the whole family continues to be actively involved with this shop, a haven for people who truly appreciate the very best.

**Schokoladen and Confiserei Holzermayr** in Alter Markt has satisfied the sweet tooth of many for over 140 years. Archduke Franz Ferdinand, who appointed Holzermayr as a supplier to the Imperial Court, shared the public enthusiasm for these sweet treats; Holzermayr was often seen pushing his handcart filled with delicious temptations in the direction of Hohenwerfen Castle.

"Chocolate for indulgence" was always the motto of the Holzermayr founder who, in addition to his business in Werfen, opened the shop on the Alter Markt in 1913 and is now in the hands of the fourth generation of his family. The interior sets a very nostalgic atmosphere with its sugar dome, a display case of chocolates and a traditional candy stand. Amongst the house specialties are the "Salzburger Mozartkugel", as well as the "Specialty Mozartkugel" for diabetics, which first appeared in 2004. The "Kids Corner" will delight children.

**Konditorei Schatz** is located in a passageway between Getreidegasse and Grunmarkt and is the smallest confectioners in the city. In 1983, Erich Winkler a master confectioner, and his wife took over the business begun by the Schatz family in 1850. As well as Mozartkugeln, customers can treat themselves to house specialties such as cherry strudel, pastries, raspberry soufflé and cherry rolls either at one of the tables in the small coffee room or opt to take home.

Café Sacher and Café Tomaselli are mentioned later in this guide, in the Restaurants section.

## Other Food Specialties

**Azwanger's** is the oldest food shop in Salzburg and during Mozart Year in 2006, celebrated its 350-year anniversary. Since its founding in 1656, the "Azwanger" on Getreidegasse, has continued to serve as a grocery store, with its antiquated shelves lending their own nostalgic flair.

The products available in this "Wine and Fancy Foods Shop" encompass an outstanding selection of the very best spirits, handmade chocolates, jams and preserves, fine vinegars and much more. Special alcohol highlights include 30-year-old whiskies, Madeira wines, fine champagnes and cognacs, as well as top wines from all over Europe.

**Sporer Wine & Spirits** is located in the narrowest house in the Getreidegasse, built in 1407. The business has been run by the Sporer family since 1903 and is now in the third and fourth generation. Today, in his grandfather's former tavern, Peter Sporer, with the help of his wife and son Michael, offers a comprehensive selection of fine distilled products stored in casks over a century old, along with 34 in house products such as 18 liqueurs with a variety of flavours which are produced on the first floor of this historic building. The "classics" include the "House Blend", a fine herbal liqueur created from old family recipes and the orange punch, made according to grandmother's original 1927 recipe.

**Kaslöchl** on Hagenauerplatz first opened in 1892 and is run today by Barbara Soukup.
Tempting displays are set out in front of the nostalgic wooden storefront for visitors to enjoy, and once you have seen what is on offer, it is impossible to resist stepping inside this tiny shop. The first thing you will notice are the very fragrant smells. Take time to look at the variety of Austrian cheeses on offer, depending on the season, the fantastic assortment can include over 120 different types of cheese, many of which are organically produced. The Trausner jams, which may be purchased here, are also a carefully guarded secret recipe. There is also a fine wine collection.

**Feinkost Kölbl** located in Mozart's former residence on the Theatergasse, is one of the last true delicatessens in Salzburg. The Kölbl family's shop was regarded, even in 1892, as one of Salzburg's leading addresses in all things culinary. After it was destroyed during the Second World War, the house was rebuilt to the original designs in 1994, and the business is now flourishing in its new splendour, without having had to surrender any of its historic character in the process. The beautifully decorated delicatessen counter tempts customers with an array of high-quality specialties: Italian hors d'oeuvres, pâtés, prosciutto from Spain, Italy and Austria, plus much more. In addition, home cooked lunch is served daily at the standing tables.

In 1879, Hungarian Ludwig Nagy set up a shop in Linzer Gasse as a gingerbread maker and chandler. The business, **Johann Nagy and Sohn**, has stayed in family hands to this day, continually expanding to now include stores all over Austria, Bavaria and even northern Italy. There are 40 different types of "Lebkuchen" gingerbread creations based on traditional recipes. A temptation hard to resist!

Today, as then, most of their products are all hand-made, this includes the drawing, pouring and dipping of candles in a broad variety of colours. The candles are then decorated with wax motifs. Their specialties include the "Wax Baby Jesus", hand-painted wax models, as well as baptismal and wedding candles.

## Other Traditional Stores

**Zur Kuchenfee** (The Kitchen Fairy) has been at the Burgherhaus at 56 Linzergasse since 1929 and claims "to have almost everything" and indeed is a treasure trove of everyday practical items. Located over 4 floors you will find everything from pots and pans, to preserving accessories to porcelain and crockery to electrical kitchen items. Many of the customers can remember coming here with their mothers and grandmothers and often turn to the shop ladies or "fairies" for their assistance in finding exactly what they need.

The traditional dress of Austria and Bavaria is known as Trachten and there are number of well renowned "Trachten" stores around the city. **Lanz Tracht** was founded in 1922 and has supplied traditional dress to artists of the Salzburg Festival as well as Elizabeth Taylor, Karl Lagerfeld, Tommy Hilfiger as well as the Royal families of Monaco, Sweden and Great Britain. **Jahn-Markl Tracht** began in 1408 and is probably Salzburg's oldest tannery, initially supplying military uniforms. Today the store is still renowned as a manufacturer of hand-made leather goods but also sells shirts, blouses and woollen clothing. **Hanna Trachten** is a relative newcomer being established in 1952. Here customers can have their Trachten and Dirndl made to measure in colours of their choice as well as choosing from the ready made range.

## Seasonal Events in Salzburg

**Highlights throughout the Year:**

**January:**
6$^{th}$ January is Epiphany and many children take part in Sternsingen, this is where they go from house to house singing and offering good luck for the year.
28$^{th}$ January is Mozart's birthday.

**February:**
Fasching – this is a festival similar to Mardi Gras and signifies the beginning of Lent. Fasching Dienstag is the day before Ash Wednesday.

**March:**
The ski season is coming to an end. March sometimes sees the inclusion of Easter and the beginning of the Easter Festival.

**April:**
Pentecost often occurs in April and this means the Salzburger Pfingstfestspiele.
23rd April is Georgitag or St Georges Day, not only is he the patron saint of England but also of horses and this is celebrated in the surrounds of Salzburg by farmers who sometimes ride the horses through the villages in traditional costume.

**May:**
Many villages raise the traditional Maibaum (maypole).
Outdoor swimming pools open and in nearby Berchtesgaden the road to the Kehlsteinhaus is opened in mid to late May.

**June:**
The weather is much better and visitors can really enjoy outdoor activities such as walking and swimming as well as relaxing in a beer garden.

**July:**
The Salzburg Festival begins.
25th July is St Jacobs Day, the patron saint of farmers and this is celebrated in outlying villages.

**August:**
The Salzburg Festival continues.
Fest in Hellbrunn takes place in the first 2 weeks of August and is a series of concerts at Hellbrunn.

**September:**
The Almabetrieb begins, this is farmers bringing the herds of cows down to the valleys from the hills, often in a great parade and the animals dressed with bells and flowers.
St Ruperts Fair

**October:**
Salzburger Kulturtage is a series of concerts and theatre performances in the city.

**November:**
1st November is All Saints Day and the graves of family loved ones will be adorned with flowers. Shops will be closed.
11th November St Martins Day is celebrated by children.
The ice skating begins at Mozartplatz and the Christkindlmarkt begins.
Late November to early January Winterfest in the Volksgarten

**December:**
Many advent activities and markets, see the chapter on the Christmas Markets later.

There are many festivals and events that occur in Salzburg throughout the year here are just a few. As you will see most of them are centred on music.

**Mozart Week**

Theatergasse 2
www.mozarteum.at

This is Salzburg's classical winter music festival and usually takes place in the last week of January. Here you can sample opera, orchestral and chamber music as well as soloists. The music played is predominantly Mozart and is a highlight for lovers of the great composer. First held in 1956, it has increased in popularity and the charm of an often snow-covered city is an added bonus.

**Easter Festival**

Founded in 1967 this festival rapidly grew to become an artistically brilliant festival. The festival begins each year on the Saturday before Palm Sunday and ends on Easter Monday. World-renowned conductors take part as well as musicians such as the Berlin Philharmonic Orchestra. Young orchestras have been given the opportunity to perform at special events since 1994.

## Salzburg Festival

www.salzburgerfestspiele.at

Ever since it was founded the Salzburg Festival has been known for its high quality of music and as a successful combination of old and new. It has greatly contributed to Salzburg's renown and is one of the world's most exclusive music festivals. It was the idea of Max Reinhardt and the first performance was on August 22, 1920 in Domplatz. Salzburg soon became the meeting point for the best directors, conductors, musicians and vocalists of the time. Today, events are held at numerous venues and include music from Africa, Asia and Europe as well as children's performances and exhibitions. The festival runs from late July through August.

## St Ruperts Fair

www.rupertikirtag.at

The traditional country fair is held on the squares surrounding Salzburg Cathedral every year in September. St. Rupert's fair, held in honour of Salzburg's patron saint, is one of the city's most popular fairs. Its farmers' market, fair booths and arcades, merry-go-rounds and carousels, Ferris wheel, Hanswurst and the suburban theatre make it a spectacular event for young and old. The fair also offers valuable insight into local customs and craftsmanship.

Each square; Domplatz, Mozartplatz, Alter Markt and Waagplatz have their own programme of events, see website for details.

## Winterfest

Volksgarten
www.winterfest.at

The idea behind the Winterfest since its inception in 2001 was to make Salzburg's Volksgarten what it once was: a venue for amazement, enjoyment and festivities.

Inspired by his visits to renowned festivals in Europe, Georg Daxner dreamt of establishing his own circus festival in Salzburg and thanks to his endless dedication, world famous circus troupes have visited Salzburg during the Winterfest, creating the only contemporary circus festival in Austria.

The philosophy behind the Winterfest is simple: to offer something special during the hectic (pre-) Christmas season: time for an evening with friends, an evening to share wonderful entertainment and enjoy a glass of wine and culinary delicacies.

Spectators in the Volksgarten will be amazed by spellbinding acrobatics, soft poetry and bizarre illusions, the shows are not loud but unique, sensational and well worth a visit.

## **Christmas Markets**

www.christkindlmarkt.co.at

10am – 8.30pm Monday – Thursday
10am – 9pm Friday
9am – 9pm Saturday
9am – 8.30pm Sunday

The Christmas Markets usually open the last week in November and run for 5 weeks to Christmas Eve.

Advent is undoubtedly one of the most beautiful seasons in the city of Salzburg. When the first snowflakes swirl in the air, children start to build snowmen in the Mirabell Gardens and the scent of mulled wine wafts through the narrow streets.

The first Christkindlmarkt was held on Residenzplatz in the fifteenth century. Today the market is centred on Residenzplatz and Domplatz and has around 100 stalls offering a wide range of goods. Visitors enjoy the welcoming ambiance whilst browsing the traditional wooden booths with their pine branch roofs. The air is filled with the enticing smells of pine needles, baked goods, incense and mulled wine.

The floral arrangements, candles and incense offer a good way to decorate your home. Textiles are available either as embroidered cloths for the table or clothing such as warm winter hats, sweaters, gloves for young and old. You can also find crafts and toys all hand made from wood that will be enjoyed by all the family. Christmas decorations will be made from glass, pewter or wood and it is possible to find any decoration you could imagine. Should you want to buy some culinary treats you can find delicious chocolates, cakes and biscuits.

To satisfy your hunger or thirst at the markets there are a number of stalls selling such delights as fruit dipped in chocolate, sausages, potatoes, schnitzels and they can all be washed down with some warming mulled wine.

At the beginning of December, around the 6$^{th}$, the squares and streets of the city are alive with Krampus and Perchten runs. Krampus is the wild, dark spirit that accompanies St Nicholas. Tradition states that Krampus will appear if children have been naughty through the year. Their traditional costumes and masks have been elaborately made by hand. The shaggy, terrifying spirits parading through the streets symbolize Perchta, a pagan alpine goddess. If you touch them or get swatted, consider yourself lucky – they are thought to bring good luck.

There is a large musical programme during advent with concerts throughout the city. Since 1946 the advent-singing programme has increased in popularity and now attracts up to 36,000 visitors each year.

You can hear informal carol singing in the markets and each evening the sound of music drifts over the market from the tops of buildings around the squares.

The carol "Silent Night" was first performed in the chapel at Oberndorf, near to Salzburg. A local pastor and teacher, composed it to help raise funds for the village chapel. Today, it has been translated into over 170 languages and is probably one of the best-known carols.

In Mozartplatz there is a large ice rink set up for people to skate upon. Here you will see people of all ages enjoying themselves on the ice. Should you be a novice there is assistance available, and it is possible to hire your skates.

If you don't want to skate but still want to enjoy the atmosphere then the Winter Lounge is for you. Here you can enjoy various flavours of warming mulled wine, hot chocolate or hot food snacks adjacent to the ice rink and the Mozart statue. Sometimes there is a large fire lit to help keep you warm too.

If you enjoy the mulled wines and punch on sale at the Winter Lounge then you can take some home. Visit the Treml shop across Mozartplatz near to Getreidegasse

**There are also smaller markets throughout the city.**

**Mirabellplatz**
10am – 8pm Sunday to Wednesday
9am – 8pm Thursday
10am – 9pm Friday & Saturday

At Mirabell Gardens, just a short walk across the river from the old town, you can browse the stalls for ceramics, wooden gifts and crafts. There are also food stalls with hot snacks, drinks and the obligatory mulled wine. There is a musical programme on Wednesdays and weekends to entertain the visitors to the market.

**Hohensalzburg Fortress**

Friday, Saturday and Sunday only

The Hohensalzburg Fortress Christmas Market is open every weekend during advent and offers spectacular views of the twinkling city below. There are craft stall and food stalls and children can make straw stars, apple men and other such things. Children will have fun making their own apple-men, straw stars, ice flowers, angels, gift tags and many other objects. Brass concerts and dance music add to the festive spirit of the season. The traditional "Christ Child Salute" by the Armed Fortress Guild takes place at noon on December 24.

**Hellbrunn Palace**

1pm – 8pm Wednesday – Friday (Monday & Tuesday too in December)
10am – 8pm Weekends

This market offers a romantic courtyard, a path lined by torches and an oversized Advent calendar are part of the Magic of Advent. Traditional booths, tempting treats and pre-Christmas gift ideas add to the charming atmosphere. Children will enjoy a ride in a sled drawn by real reindeer. An entertainment programme will assure that Advent afternoons at Hellbrunn Palace are enjoyable.

**Sterngarten**

In the courtyard at the Sternbräu, the Sterngarten is a hidden little treasure. Here there are a handful of stalls offering arts and crafts. All proceeds are donated to charity.

## **Food and Drink in Salzburg and Bavaria**

The food and drink of Salzburg and Bavaria is very similar – hearty, home cooked, a consistently high standard and delicious. There is a great deal of choice in the area, numerous small cafes for snacks, traditional restaurants for lunch or dinner and even a la carte dining in 5-star hotels. Many restaurants offer a "Tageskarte" or daily special which is available at lunchtimes. Be prepared to share your table with strangers, most restaurants have traditional large tables which seat up to 12 and it is common practice to sit more than one group of people at these tables.

For light meals and snacks you will find soups, salads and cold meat, sausage and cheese platters. Alternatively, you can enjoy the Austrian and German tradition of coffee and cake in a café.
For main meals you can choose from steaks, crispy roast pork, and spicy goulash with noodles, Wiener Schnitzel or a crispy pork knuckle. Seasonal side salads are the usual accompaniment as opposed to vegetables.

Desserts include apple strudel and Kaiserschmarrn (chopped pancake served with fruit and usually for 2 people). In most bars and restaurants you will find that the beer will be from the local brewery, is served cold and tastes good. Schnapps will often be from the local distillery at Grassl.

Local specialties include crispy Wiener Schnitzel, a veal or pork escalope in breadcrumbs fried and served with potatoes or fries. Although not invented in Vienna, the breaded and fried veal escalope has long become one of the city's famous icons.

Tafelspitz is a popular boiled beef dish that can be served with green vegetables and potatoes.

Kasespaetzle is the Austrian and Bavarian version of macaroni cheese. Noodles served hot with a delicious cheese sauce is just the dish for a cold day, filling and delicious and often served with crispy fried onions on top.

For those with a sweet tooth you will always find apple strudel on menus, layers of crisp filo pastry filled with juicy apples, raisins and sometimes chopped nuts served warm with either ice cream or vanilla sauce. Almost a meal in itself.

The original Sachertorte has been the most famous cake in the world since 1832 and the original recipe remains a well-kept secret of the Sacher Hotel in Salzburg. The basis of this delicious confection is a rich chocolate cake, thinly coated with apricot jam and the chocolate icing on top of the cake is the crowning glory. It tastes best with a portion of unsweetened whipped cream.

The Salzburger Nockerl is a light and fluffy dessert that may remind some people of Salzburg's snow-capped-mountains, but it is definitely a real treat for dessert lovers. The dessert is usually served in portions for two people. Legend has it that the famous Salzburg prince archbishop of Raitenau loved his mistress Salome mainly because of her exquisite Salzburger Nockerl.

Linzer Torte is considered by many Austrians to be the oldest cake in the World. The oldest version of the Linzer Torte recipe comes from a cookbook that is over 350 years old; even at this early date, the cookbook already included four different recipes for the Linzer Torte, proof for how popular and widely known the cake was already.

Kaiserschmarrn is a dessert served in portions for two. It consists of chopped pancake with raisins usually served with a portion of fruit sauce on the side. It is very filling.

**Food Dictionary**

Here are some of the typical things you will find on the menu; many main restaurants will have English menus.

Schweinebraten – Roast Pork
Schweinhaxe – Pork Knuckle
Rostbraten – Steak
Hendl – Chicken
Forelle – Trout
Lachs – Salmon
Bratkartoffeln – Roast Potatoes
Knödel – Dumplings (either potato or bread)
Bayerische Crème – A creamy dessert
Apfelkuchen – Apple Cake
Windbeutel – A large cream puff filled with ice cream and served with cream and fruit

## Places to Eat in Salzburg

There are a great number of cafes, bars and restaurants in Salzburg to suit all tastes and price ranges, from shady beer gardens to coffee houses or gourmet restaurants.

**Café Sacher**

Schwarzstrasse 5

Located in the Hotel Sacher near to the Mirabell Gardens this café is home to the famous Sachertorte. Inside is a traditional coffee house and in summer you can sit on the terrace that overlooks the river. Recommended to accompany Sachertorte is a "Pharisäer" coffee, which has a shot of rum. The story of the origins of this coffee go back to the nineteenth century when the local priest berated his congregation on the evils of drink and called them "Pharisees", this led the congregation to hide their rum in the coffee and top it with cream. There is a small store that is part of the hotel that sells Sachertorte to take away.

## Café Tomaselli

Alter Markt 9

Founded in 1705 this is Austria's oldest "Viennese" coffee house, and the style has not changed much in 300 years. The walls are laid with wood panelling, marble tables and waiters and waitresses will serve you on silver trays. You can choose from a selection of coffees and over 40 homemade cakes that are baked fresh daily. Taste the different coffee variations such as Melange (a mix of frothed milk and steamed coffee), Grosser Brauner (a large cup of steamed black coffee), Verlängerter (a larger but weaker version of the Grosser Brauner, typically served with milk) or Einspänner (strong, black coffee served in a high glass with a dash of whipped cream). Many famous people including Mozart and Max Reinhardt have frequented this café. In warmer weather you can sit on the balcony or the "Kiosk" which is an outdoor café garden first used in 1860

## Sternbräu

Griesgasse 23
www.sternbrau.com
The restaurant is also accessed from Getreidegasse.

This restaurant has been here for 600 years and you can choose from 5 restaurants set out in 14 rooms, so each time you eat here you feel as if you are in a different restaurant.
In the function room you can see the "Sound of Salzburg Show" which features songs from the Sound of Music. The performers are dressed in traditional clothes and there is a short film that features Maria von Trapp. This can be accompanied by a dinner. Bookings can be made at the above website. The shows are on from May to October.

In the inner courtyard at Christmas is a small Christmas market. At other times children can play here.

## StieglKeller

Festungsgasse 10
www.imlauer.com

Nestled under the Hohensalzburg this restaurant offers fantastic views of the city and in summer has one of the best beer gardens in Salzburg. The three outdoor terraces offer seating for over 300 people. However there is plenty of seating indoors in a variety of rooms, which have a welcoming feel that accompanies the friendly welcome of the staff. The food is Austrian and you can try the local Stiegl beer.

## StieglBräu

Rainerstrasse 14
www.imlauer.com

The centrally located StieglBräu Restaurant in Salzburg is not only popular with guests from all over the world but also with the locals. The reason, of course, is the cuisine. Traditional home-style Austrian food is served and, to accompany it, you should order an excellent Stiegl beer. The StieglBräu Restaurant menu offers you a rich choice of various classic Austrian dishes such as the Wiener Schnitzel to sweet desserts of Austrian pastry confections, everything that could possibly tempt you.

## Stein Hotel

Giselakai

This hotel has a fabulous rooftop bar and restaurant. In the summer you can sit beneath umbrellas to protect you from the sun and in winter (If there is not too much snow) sit wrapped up in blankets with heaters at your table. You can have just a coffee and cake during the day or maybe a full lunch or evening meal. Whatever you choose the views of the city are amazing.

## Augustiner Bräu

Augustinerbräustrasse 4
www.augustinerbier.at

If you have been to Munich you will know how industrious the monks were in brewing beer and it is no different here. They began brewing in 1621 and the beer is still flowing. Indoor is a large beer hall with wooden tables and chairs that can sit up to 1400 people, so plenty of room for all.

In the summer months the beer garden will sit up to 1600 guests who want to make the most of the warmer temperatures. The food is Austrian and delicious.

## Zwettlers Stiftskeller

Kaigasse 3
www.zwettlers.com
Tuesday to Saturday 11.30am – 2am
Sunday 11.30am – 11pm
Closed Monday except during August and December

Under new ownership since 2011, this traditional bar and restaurant serves Kaiser Karl beer direct "vom Fass" or wooden barrel. The house specialty is the "Zwickl" beer which is served natural and unfiltered. The Weissbier is also highly recommended and features in cocktails too. The menu has all the favourites you would expect including schnitzels, goulash and grills.

## K&K Restaurant
Waagplatz 2

The building was originally a Merchants house and is easy to find being centrally located next to the Dom. Seating indoors is spread through the 9 rooms or Stübe and outdoors the courtyard will accommodate 120 guests. The food is traditionally Austrian.

Gablerbrau
Linzer Gasse 9

This is the most historical beer tavern on the right bank and has been here since 1429. Renovated in 2013 it still remains its cosy and welcoming feel with wooden furniture, floors and walls, stained glass windows and traditional stoves. The food is reasonably priced, traditionally Austrian featuring favourites such as goulash, Schnitzel and Tafelspitz. A children's menu is available.

# Day Trips from Salzburg

## Wolfgangsee

South of Salzburg is Wolfgangsee, one of the most beautiul lakes in Austria. On it's shores are the pretty towns of St Gilgen, St Wolfgang and Strobl. In the summer the area is popular for hiking, cycling, climbing , horse riding, fishing and swimming and many other sports. The area is popular for skiing and winter sports once the first snows have fallen.

You can take boat trips on the lake to visit each of the towns and enjoy a unique view of the scenery. The "Emperor Franz Joseph I" paddle steamer first set sail on the Wolfgangsee in 1873 and heralded the beginning of a scheduled service on the Wolfgangsee. The 33-metre nostalgic ship has been featured in a number of films and continues to be part of the fleet. Today the fleet has six cruisers with the "Wolfgang Amadeus" the flagship, the "Österreich" is the largest ship. A trip on the renovated "Kaiserschiff" is an experience reminiscent of the Imperial and Royal Monarchy. The cruises operate all year round, although the service is adapted to the individual seasons. The stops include: St. Gilgen - Fürberg - Ried/Falkenstein - Schafberg Railroad - St. Wolfgang - Geschwendt parking lot - Strobl.

The town of St Gilgen has a pretty centre with some shops and restaurants. It is famous for being the birthplace of Mozart's mother in 1720 and the Mozart House is used today for concerts and exhibitions.

Strobl is reputed to have the flattest shoreline along the lake and is connected to the other towns by boat trip. It nestles right up to the lake edge and it's baroque church stands out as a landmark as you approach.

St Wolfgang has a beautiful town centre with market place and is most famous for the starting point for the Schafbergbahn Cog Railway. This is the steepest cog railway in Austria, the forty-minute ride journeys 6 kilometres up to an altitude of 1,190 metres and offers breath taking views. Since 1893, the steam locomotives have been taking visitors to the mountain summit in order that they can take in the views and scenery of the Alpine lakes and as far as the Dachstein Glacier. Once you have reached the top you can have some refreshments at Austria's oldest mountain inn, the Hotel Schafbergspitze, opened in 1862. The railway operates from April to October depending on the weather and is

particularly good fun for families.
From St Wolfgang you can also hike over the Falkenstein to St Gilgen

## Hallein Salt Mines

The salt mine in the Dürrnberg near Hallein was a source of Salzburg's wealth, salt often being referred to as "white gold". Visitors climb aboard the mine train for a comfortable, fun-filled ride into the centre of the mountain, where two long miners' slides take you down to an underground salt lake. A new multi-media show now takes you into a magical world of light and sound and the history of "White Gold". You can follow in the footsteps of the Ancient Celts, who had been mining salt here since 400 B.C., and discover the mysterious world of the miners themselves who, with their bare hands, dug deep into the mountain. Today's visitors, big and small, can look forward to adventure, fascinating insights and all kinds of fun during the tour.

This family activity is great fun whatever the weather.

## Werfen

The castle of Hohenwerfen has towered over the 155 metre high craggy rock above the Salzachtal valley for more than 900 years. The strong fortifications were built at the same time as Hohensalzburg Fortress and are some of the best preserved late medieval defences and rooms in Europe. Over the centuries they have seen countless attacks and sieges, and several great rulers and lords, such as Archbishop Wolf Dietrich von Raitenau, were held prisoner in the castle.

A tour of the castle includes a walk around the castle chapel, the kitchen, the armoury and arsenal featuring an exhibition of the weapons over the ages, the battlements, the bell tower and the rooms of the regents. Hohenwerfen Fortress stages a wide range of year round events, trails, evening tours, falconry demonstrations, and at Christmas an Advent market.

The Hohenwerfen Fortress was used by the archbishops of Salzburg as a hunting base demonstrated by the existence of the falconry centre. As well as the 'Landesfalkenhof' the castle is also home to Austria's very first museum of falconry featuring a special educational trail for those interested in learning about birds of prey. There are daily demonstrations of the high art of falconry as practised in a number of countries to this day.

A totally new mountain experience is a visit to the largest ice caves in the world. Travel by one of Austria's steepest cable car rides to the huge entrance of the caves, measuring 20 metres wide and 18 metres high, that can be seen from quite a distance. In this wintry world of ice, the system of caves stretches for over 42 kilometres, the first kilometre features gigantic ice formations, and you will also see beautiful ice palaces, even on hot summer days. This part is open to the public and can be viewed only on a guided tour.

Please note:
Access to the caves takes 20 minutes on foot to the cable car and after getting out from the cable car it is another 20 minutes on foot to the entrance of the caves (1642 metres). It is then another climb of 134 metres via 1400 steps in the caves themselves.

**Top Tip:**
The caves have an average temperature of 0° C, even throughout the summer months, warm clothing and sturdy shoes required.

**Lokwelt**
Freilassing

This railway museum is an extension of the Deutsches Museum in Munich. Here you will find over 150 years of railway history. Located in an old railway depot on rail tracks between Munich and Salzburg the museum has attracted over 40,000 visitors since it's opening in 2006. For younger visitors (6 – 12 years) "Little Lokwelt" is focused on bringing the railway to life for them in a colourful and interactive way. New to the museum is the locomotive simulator where young and old can live out their dreams to be an engine driver.

**Mautendorf Castle**
Mautendorf
About 90 minutes' drive from Salzburg

In centuries gone by various valuable goods made their way along the old Roman trading routes over the Tauern mountains; commodities such as salt, wheat, wine and spices. These were treacherous times for the merchants, unpredictable weather, dangerous terrain and thieves and there was no way of avoiding the toll duties charged at Mautendorf Castle. The path led directly through the toll gate, the existence of which was first documented in 1002 AD.

Today, Mautendorf Castle is an impressive monument to the building achievements of the past, housing a very rich history within its walls. On a tour with an audio guide, visitors encounter life-size models like the archbishop in a hot tub, a group of medieval musicians, and the horse and cart in the courtyard. There is also fun to be had with the medieval clothing that visitors are given the opportunity to try on. Mauternburg is one of the three well-preserved toll stations along the famous 'Via Imperialis', and also offers fascinating features such as the Lungau country museum, the cosy restaurant tavern, a large medieval games area and several events, making it an ideal destination for outings for the whole family.

The 700 year old lookout, the Peel Tower is 44 metres high, unique in Europe in its design and provides a fantastic view of the Lungau region. The uses of the tower in the past are authentically displayed on the six floors including the weaponry and ammunition depots, the living area with a cooking facility, a food store room, emergency quarters and a place for the guards and inhabitants to relax.

## The Grossglockner Alpine World

www.grossglockner.at

The Grossglockner is one of the most famous alpine roads, situated in the heart of the Hohe Tauern National Park. The Grossglockner Mountain itself reaches a height of almost 3,800 metres.

The road is the ultimate driving experience that features a vintage car rally each summer, you travel along 48 kilometres, ascend to the Hochtor, the highest point, at an altitude of 2,504 metres by passing round 36 bends. The scenery is breath-taking; mountains, alpine meadows, mountain forests, rugged cliffs and year round ice. There is a view point at the Fuscher Tori with Clemens-Holzmeister memorial and also at the Kaiser-Franz-Josefs-Hohe where there is a visitor's centre.

The visitors centre features permanent and special exhibitions, the Glockner cinema, the Wilhelm Swarovski Observatory and the

Garnsgruben Trail, an interactive presentation of the mountain and the Pasterze Glacier.

Please note that this is a toll road and access is weather permitting.

## Krimml Worlds of Water

www.wasserwunderwelten.at
1 May – 31 October 9.30am – 5pm.

The Wondrous Worlds of Water welcomes visitors to a new experience, follow the streams of the Hohe Tauern and experience water in a unique way. The newly opened Waterfall Centre is the ideal place from which to visit the Krimml Waterfalls.

Features of the Waterfall Centre include the Aquascenarium, a panoramic terrace with great views, including a 3D telescope to see the Falls and a cafe and gift shop.

The House of Water exhibition explains why the Hohe Tauern area is renowned for relieving the symptoms of asthma.

The Wondrous Works of Water is an outdoor area that enables every visitor, young or old, to interact with water.

**Top Tip:**
Combination tickets for all attractions available only at the Waterfall Centre.

# **Berchtesgaden**

Nestling in the South East of the German Alps in the Berchtesgadener Land National Park, the town is popular with locals and tourists all year round. Located just 30 kilometres from Salzburg and 180 kilometres from Munich, Berchtesgaden is easily accessible. It is surrounded by Mount Watzmann, Germany's third highest mountain, the Kehlstein and nearby is the glacial lake of Königssee.

There are 8 prominent mountain peaks that surround Berchtesgaden; the Karkopf (1738 metres) which is popular in the summer for hiking; Hochkalter (2607 metres) situated west of the Watzmann in the National Park; Hochstaufen (1771 metres) the easternmost mountain in the Bavarian Alps; Hoher Göll (2522 metres) the highest of the Gölls and first climbed in 1800; Stadel Horn (2286 metres) located on the border between Bavaria and Salzburg; Grosses Teufelshorn (2362 metres) the highest peak in the Hagengebirge and the afore mentioned Watzmann at 2713 metres.

There are a variety of sights and sports to be either watched or tried at all times of the year, whatever the weather. Several of the visitor attractions in Berchtesgaden are listed in the German National Tourist Board's Top 100 attractions and these include Lake Königssee, St Bartholoma, the Kehlsteinhaus, Salzbergwerk and the Berchtesgaden National Park. The Berchtesgaden area is an ideal holiday destination, whether you are a couple looking for a peaceful, picturesque location or a family who wants to make the most of the sights and the sports that are on offer.

## History

It was around 700AD when Bavarian Prince Theodo made the gift of some grazing lands to the founder of Salzburg, Bishop Rupert that we first here of the area. Berchtesgaden got its first real mention in the history books in the eleventh century when the area was a popular hunting ground for Lord Perther of Salzburg. He enjoyed the area so much he built himself a small lodge to stay in, a "Gaden" and this became known as "Perther's Gaden" and the origin of the name Berchtesgaden. In 1190 the power of the local community grew because of the local salt mines, from which the area has continued to receive a great deal of its wealth. The area came under Bavarian rule in1810 and was very popular with the Bavarian Royal Family who enjoyed the lake and had a hunting lodge here.

The Royal Family continued to favour Berchtesgaden for over 100 years, until 1933 when Hitler came to power. The Nazi party had purchased the area in the 1930's for the Nazi leaders to enjoy and their infamous leader, Adolf Hitler, resided in the Berghof on the Obersalzberg. He was given the Kehlsteinhaus in 1939 for his birthday. The Berchtesgaden area was in the American sector after the end of the war and is now owned by the State of Bavaria. The National Park was established in 1978.

## Weather

The weather in Berchtesgaden is deeply influenced by the Alps. The winters are cold, temperatures often not getting above freezing from November to February and snowfall is possible from November onwards. Mild spring days are common but with chilly evenings. In summer the weather is warm, with temperatures in the 20's from June until August. Autumn is much the same as spring.

## Berchtesgaden Town Centre

The citizens of Berchtesgaden can be proud of their town centre. Many historic buildings have been preserved and the alpine tradition of fresco painting on the building walls is much in evidence. Walking tours of the historic town centre can be taken both day and night and in winter the tour is carried out by torch flame. Tour details can be found at the Tourist

Information opposite the Hauptbahnhof (train station) or at the Kur and Kongress building in town centre. You can also take your own walk using the guide later in this guide. The central pedestrian area of the town presents the opportunity for a stroll around the many shops or enjoying a coffee or drink and watching the world go by. A weekly market is held on Fridays on Weihnachtsschützenplatz, in the pedestrian area.

There are numerous shops offering a great variety of goods. The sports stores stock all the items you need for whatever the season – ski suits and skis in winter or hiking boots and sticks in summer. There are craft shops selling trinkets and souvenirs of the area, and many photographic books of the fantastic local scenery. You should also check out the wood carving stores such as Holzschnitzerei Huber, as woodcarving was a major industry in the area from the 1500's and continues today and is the second largest woodcarving producing area in Germany. There are also shops selling chocolates, delicatessens and wine stores selling local produce and gifts. Trachten (the local Bavarian dress) is available in stores too and is still widely worn by locals, and the heavy woollen winter coats are designed to protect against the cold temperatures. Shops are generally open 9am to 6pm Monday to Friday, close at 4pm on Saturday, although some may close for lunch. All shops are closed on Sunday.
www.berchtesgaden.de

## **Berchtesgaden and the Bavarian Royal Family**

### King Maximilian I (reigned 1799 – 1825)
It was in 1818 that Maximilian I first began the close links between the Wittelsbach dynasty and Berchtesgaden. He proved himself to be well educated and a practical leader and the locals welcomed him with open arms. He chose the Castle as his summer residence and this and Königssee became the royals' favourite holiday home. His favourite past time was hunting in the forests and he often came home with large numbers of game and deer (maybe because the gamekeepers had prevented the animals from escaping and therefore made the kill easier). Maximilian also supported the community, when in 1820 the salt works were destroyed by fire he ordered the reconstruction and thus guaranteeing the livelihoods of a large part of the locals.

### King Ludwig I (reigned 1825 – 1848)
Ludwig I was a much different ruler than his father and he believed in a strongly monarchist approach with the ruler exercising control over

subjects, where his father had been much gentler and patient. This does not mean however that he was not liked. He, like his parents loved the Berchtesgaden area and he would visit for holidays just as they had done. He also took an interest in local affairs and was responsible for the building of a hospital in the area. He had a number of interests; firstly art mainly brought about by his time in Italy and he commissioned many paintings. His second interest was women, and this is demonstrated by the paintings of his favourites in Schloss Nymphenburg in Munich. It was his last love that caused his downfall as she tried to influence the Court and he was forced to step down in favour of his son. However, he is probably most famous for his marriage to Princess Therese in 1810 and the wedding celebrations that are still held every year in Munich – "Oktoberfest".

**King Maximilian II (reigned 1848 - 1864)**
Maximilian was a strong and responsible king with a concern for the poor. He travelled all over Europe and made it his duty to enhance Munich and Bavaria's reputation. He brought leading scientists, poets and authors to the area to seek their knowledge and advice. He was also a builder, and as well as many buildings in Munich he commissioned a new home in Berchtesgaden, the Königliche Villa (Royal Villa), a mix of Roman and Bavarian styles. He loved spending time at this new home with his wife and 2 sons and hunting in the forests as his predecessors had done. He also enjoyed riding in the area and ensured that the existing walking paths were well maintained as well as creating new ones.

**King Ludwig II (reigned 1864 – 1886)**
Ludwig II is probably Bavaria's most famous King, also known as the "mad King" or "Dream King" he was responsible for the building of the fairy-tale castle such as Neuschwanstein and Herrenchiemsee. He and his brother, Otto, spent many of their childhood summers in Berchtesgaden, however they were kept very much in the background and not seen as part of the Royal party. Ludwig celebrated his seventeenth birthday with a cruise on Königssee and later on when King, he saved the church at St Bartholoma from demolition. After his accession to the throne Ludwig did not visit Berchtesgaden again, however the "Salt Grotto" at the salt mines is a tribute to his memory.

**Prince Regent Luitpold (ruled 1886 -1912)**
After the sudden death of Ludwig II, his uncle Luitpold became Prince Regent, as there were no heirs to the throne. This was a calm period in Bavaria's history and thus Luitpold was able to spend a lot of time in

Berchtesgaden, however he preferred the Schloss to the Royal Villa. He particularly enjoyed hunting and horse riding, even in to his late 80's. He would spend many a night in the hunting lodges at St Bartholoma, Hintersee and the Wimbach valley. The Prince Regent was very popular with the locals and greatly missed after his death.

### King Ludwig III (reigned 1912 -1918)

Ludwig III ascended to the throne late in his life, and his reign would be very short, but like his father before him enjoyed the Berchtesgaden area very much. When in 1918, an uprising headed by Kurt Eisner, flared up in Munich, Ludwig and his family were advised to flee; they headed for Berchtesgaden and the hunting lodge at Hintersee. The locals kept them supplied with food and clothes and kept their whereabouts as secret as they could. However, it was soon discovered that revolutionaries were headed their way and they moved closer to the Austrian border, to Schloss Anif, but they were soon discovered there too. The King was advised to abdicate but he managed to work out a deal where he renounced the throne but the family could remain and travel around Bavaria of their own free will. Once the deal was agreed, Ludwig and his family returned to Königssee to adjust to their new life.

### Crown Prince Rupprecht (1869 – 1955)

Rupprecht loved the Berchtesgaden area and after his marriage in 1900, he and his wife Marie Gabriele spent a lot of time here. His wife was not in good health but the clear mountain air was good for her. They had 5 children but only 1 survived through to adulthood and Marie Gabriele herself died young, at the age of 34. Rupprecht remarried and he and his new wife, Antonia, spent much time restoring the Schloss and building an impressive art collection. However this idyllic lifestyle was to come to an end with the beginning of the Nazi era. Hitler viewed Rupprecht as a threat because he was still loved by the people, so the Schloss was requisitioned and Rupprecht and his family forced to flee. They were eventually captured and placed in a concentration camp and when rescued by American troops it is said that Antonia was close to death. After the war, Rupprecht returned to Berchtesgaden and in 1955 his daughter was married in the town.

Today, members of the Wittelsbach family continue to visit Berchtesgaden and stay in a private wing of the Schloss.

# **Berchtesgaden and the Third Reich**

Hitler first visited the area with his friend Dietrich Eckart in mid-1923 and he stayed on the Obersalzberg, declaring the area "completely captivating". He was arrested shortly afterwards in Munich for his role in the Beer Hall Putsch and imprisoned in Landshut. On his release in late 1924, Hitler returned to the Obersalzberg and in 1927 he rented Haus Wachenfeld, which gave him stunning views of the valley and towards his home country, Austria. He was later to remark, "those were the best days of my life". Whilst here he gave talks to small groups and completed writing Mein Kampf.

In 1933 when Hitler became Chancellor he purchased Haus Wachenfeld and began its expansion and transformation into The Berghof. Hitler entertained many heads of state here including British Prime Ministers Lloyd George and Neville Chamberlain, Ambassadors and foreign ministers, the Aga Khan and the Duke and Duchess of Windsor. The Nazi Party also began to purchase neighbouring land from farmers, initially at generous prices but latterly not so, in order to create the Obersalzberg complex. Between 1923 and 1936 Hitler spent up to 6 months a year at his alpine retreat, here many decisions about the war were made. During this time the mountain became a tourist attraction for those wanting to catch a glimpse of their leader and thus the mountain became heavily restricted and closed off to all except the chosen few. The party propaganda machine used these images of the Führer and his people to portray him as a friend, lover of nature and children.

From 1936, under the direction of Martin Bormann, a vast building programme was undertaken. A new road from Berchtesgaden was built and facilities such as SS Barracks, staff living quarters, childcare and food and recreation buildings were created. These were all heavily guarded and protected. Other party leaders such as Göring and Bormann himself also acquired homes on the mountain. The Eagles Nest was built high on top of the mountain for Hitler as his fiftieth birthday present but in fact he preferred the teahouse at Mooslahnerkopf.

As the war progressed the fear of air raids became stronger and it was decided to dig a series of underground bunkers for safety. This was a huge undertaking that was never quite completed. In 1945 when the Allies carried out air raids on the mountain, much of the complex was extensively damaged including the Berghof but not the Eagles Nest. The buildings that survived were then utilised by the Americans after the war and today a Documentation Centre detailing the history of the Obersalzberg stands where the Platterhof hotel was on the complex.

After the war, the Obersalzberg was overshadowed by its role during the war. Many discussions were held between the authorities and the locals as to how to develop the area. Whilst some were in favour of agriculture, many wanted to return to the high-class tourism days of pre 1933. The Obersalzberg area was occupied by the Americans and the locals were banned from the area until 1949, however that did not prevent some opportunists from showing visitors the highlights including the Berghof, for a substantial fee. After the banning order was lifted, people came here not only for historical reasons but also for the beauty of the area. The Kehlsteinhaus was reopened in 1952.

## Documentation Obersalzberg

The Documentation Centre on the Obersalzberg is a permanent exhibition that details the story of the town and the mountain during the reign of the Third Reich. The area was Hitler's mountain retreat and therefore was visited by many dignitaries including politicians from all over the World, as well as Nazi Party leaders. There are many photographs and scale models to show you where everything was located. You can proceed through the exhibition, at your own pace, using an audio guide that can be hired at the entrance in a number of languages. There is a map showing the location of the bunkers and it is possible to walk through some of this vast network of tunnels that still exist deep into the mountain. This is the first extensive presentation of what took place during the Nazi era and the information is presented in a straightforward, factual and historical manner. The Documentation Centre is well signposted from the town if you are travelling by car; alternatively there is a local bus. The Centre attracts over 250,000 visitors each year. There is a souvenir shop and restaurant at the car park/ bus stop and guides of the Documentation can be bought at the Centre entrance.

**The Bunker Complex**

Construction began on the bunkers in 1943 but was never part of the main "Alpine Fortress". The Berghof had its own bunker complex from where the leaders could continue to rule if the buildings above ground were destroyed. There were 6 main sections of bunkers connected to each other by long corridors and each of these represented the main above ground buildings. The workers and employees bunkers were only short-term air raid shelters. Ironically, when the air raid eventually began in 1945, it was not the party officials who survived but the 1000 or so workers in their short-term shelter. The bunker complex is accessed from the Documentation Centre.

**The Kehlsteinhaus (Eagles Nest)**

Ranked a German National Tourist Board "Top 100 Sights in Germany"

The Eagle's Nest was a present to Adolf Hitler from the Nazi leaders on his fiftieth birthday, although for various reasons, including his fear of heights, he rarely visited. At a height of just over 6000 feet, you can get some breath taking views from the top, up to 125 miles on a clear day. It was an incredible feat of engineering, even by today's standards.

First, you take a special bus from next to the Documentation Centre; the journey lasts about 15 minutes and takes you up the single-track Eagle's Nest Road. The road was completed in just over a year, being blasted from rock and clinging to the side of the mountain. From here you enter a stone tunnel that takes you 400 feet inside the mountain. Now you step inside an elegant brass elevator that can hold up to 40 people, that takes you the remaining 407 feet to the top, in less than a minute. The building itself is now a restaurant, but the views are spectacular. The majority of the original furnishings were looted after the war and the large oak buffet in the dining room is the only piece of original furniture that remains.

The Eagle's Nest was not bombed during the war, despite many attempts. After the war the building was saved from demolition by the personal intervention of the District President and this enables us to see this historic monument as it was originally built. Today it is owned by the State of Bavaria and is managed by the Tourist Office of the Berchtesgadener Land. The Eagle's Nest attracts over a ¼ million visitors each year.
Every spring volunteers from the tourist office and local mountain groups check and clean the rock face on the Eagle's Nest Road, as many stones become loose over the hard winter. These loose stones could be dangerous to the buses and passengers should there be a rock fall.

The Kehlsteinhaus is open from mid-May to early October, depending on the weather. The buses leave the car park at regular intervals from about 8.30am to 4pm. Guided tours can be booked in town. Occasionally you can book dinner in the restaurant and this includes historical talks about the building.

## Berghof Ruins

After you have visited either the Documentation Centre or have been to the Eagles Nest a short walk will take you to the ruins of the Berghof, Hitler's main house on the Obersalzberg. These are not sign-posted but as you drive up the Obersalzberg take a turn to the left to the Kempinski Hotel. Just before you reach the hotel you will pass the Hotel Zum Türken on your right, here you can also take tours of the bunkers located here. Park your car and walk back down the road for about 20 or 30 metres. There is a track on the left- hand side, walk along for about 50 metres and you will see some large boulders that are now overgrown, this is all that is left of the Berghof. The final remains of the Berghof were blown up in 1952. Standing here you can imagine the fantastic views that would have greeted any visitor to this mountain hideaway.

It is also worth noting that the Kempinski Hotel was the site of Hermann Göring's house and the pond with ornamental fish was originally his swimming pool. There were many miles of tunnels in these mountains and a great many valuable items such as paintings were stored here by the Third Reich for safety.

The ski and golf club at the Gutshof was known as the Platterhof after the war and this is where the US troops were stationed.

## Towns and Lakes

There are what is known as the 5 communities in the area; Berchtesgaden, Ramsau, Bischofsweisen, Markt Schellenberg and Schönau.

### Schönau

Located on the lakeside at Königssee, Schönau has been here since 1810. Many of the activities of the town are sports focused such as skiing, the lake and Mount Jenner for walking and skiing. There are a number of nice restaurants either by the lake or in the town itself, just a few minutes away. In the area by the lake there are a number of small souvenir shops, Trachten shops and craft shops. You can take many walks in the area. The town climbs up to the pastures above and describes itself as "Fit for a King". There are many small hotels and guesthouses around the town.

### Ramsau

This alpine village is in a setting that is nature at its best. Ramsau is in a secluded valley within the Berchtesgaden basin. The Watzmann Mountain and Hochkalter range are the southern walls and the western Reiteralpe range form a border to Austria while the Latterngebirge form a protection from the north. The river "Ramsauer Ache" flows through Ramsau. This forms the only valley exit to the east, towards Berchtesgaden. The three mountain pass roads of Schwarzbachwacht, Hirschbichl and Hochschwarzeck also form routes out of the village.

Ramsau was an important point on the trading map due to its location. It is situated along the path over the Hirschbichl Pass and on to Pinzgau, an area in Austria. Ramsau became part of Bavaria along with Berchtesgaden in the reforms of 1818 and established itself as a village. Ramsau became well known to the gentry due to its excellent hunting grounds.

Artists have been coming here for centuries to capture the local area; the turquoise of nearby Hintersee, the "Blue Ice" glacier, the Wimbach gorge waterfall and the picturesque church. In winter skating and curling are possible on Hintersee and in summer you can rent a rowing boat. The church was built in 1512 and it is not only a symbol for Ramsau but it is often used to represent this alpine area. In summer there are 114 miles of paths and tracks for walkers and in winter, the usual winter sports are available.

## Bischofsweisen

In summer the flower covered meadows area delight and in winter this town is renowned for the winter sports available. The Naturbad Aschauerweiher is in this township and is popular for swimming in summer and skating and cross-country skiing in winter. The large ski area of Götschen is nearby and can offer floodlit skiing 2 nights a week. Occasionally it is possible to watch World Cup skiing here.

## Markt Schellenberg

Located on the road between Salzburg and Berchtesgaden this small town was known long ago for refining salt. Marble has been quarried from Mount Untersberg since 1683, and still has Germany's last marble mill. The mill is open in the summer months and there is also a gift shop and an inn for refreshments. It is possible to take the cable car to the top of Mount Untersberg. You can walk from the town to see the ice caves of Untersberg in the summer months. The area has many country inns and farms; farm holidays make the area popular with families.

There are several other small towns and villages in the area such as Maria Gern, with its beautiful church that are worth a look. Perhaps you may want to take a trip along the Rossfeld Road, which takes you high up into the mountains and you can look out over the valleys of Salzburg and Berchtesgaden.

**Bad Reichenhall**

Bad Reichenhall is a spa town where visitors enjoy a relaxing holiday in a quiet and impressive atmosphere. The town offers spa and health facilities as well as historic and classic events and beautiful parks. Bad Reichenhall has an historic city centre for you to explore as well as museums such as the Alte Saline (Old Salt Mines).

Much of the town of Bad Reichenhall is supplied with drinking water from the Nonner Oberland. The water is pumped from 3 wells and naturally fed into the drinking water system, therefore the tap water is pure mountain spring water. The ideal geological, hydrogeological and climatic conditions of Bad Reichenhall enable it to tap large reserves of drinking water of the highest quality from the mountain region. The most important quality characteristic of Bad Reichenhall water is the high oxygen content. The naturally oxygenated water is ideal in preventative medicine and remedies, in addition to sports medicine.

Bad Reichenhall, is famous as a spa town and was named the first "German Alpine Wellness Location". In 2001, Bad Reichenhall received the title Alpine City of the Year. A centrepiece in Bad Reichenhall's wellness atmosphere is the Spa & Fitness Resort Rupertus Therme. This glamorous and quiet spa resort is the perfect location for relaxation and regeneration.

Bad Reichenhall successfully combines day and night activities. After an interesting and relaxing day visitors can enjoy cultural highlights such as a concert from the philharmonic orchestra or a classic event in a unique atmosphere.

**Anger**

King Ludwig I once declared that Anger was the "most beautiful" village in his kingdom. The landmark of this town is its village square with its column of the Virgin Mary erected in 1884, the gold-clad patron saint of

Bavaria towers into the sky. Kloster Höglwörth, once an abbey of Augustinian monks, was founded in 1125. In Anger the old traditions have not changed much throughout the centuries with their folk dances, Schuhplattler (thigh slapping dances) and traditional Trachten dress which are still today very much part of daily life.

## Laufen

The transport of salt on the Salzach and Saalach Rivers brought the town of Laufen riches and recognition. The filigree bridge between Laufen (Germany) and Oberndorf (Austria) was built between 1902 and 1903 across the river Salzach and as one of the few remaining Art Nouveau bridges in Germany, it is now protected by the historical preservation society.

The old Rathaus or town hall in Laufen dates back to the 15th century. On the first floor you should take a look at the magnificent Gothic arch and on the second floor have a look at the beautifully restored baroque Alter Rathaussaal, which has been called Rottmayrsaal since 2004. This hall displays the impressive Rottmayr painting 'Allegorie der Astronomie und Geschichtswissenschaft' from 1710.

## Rossfeld

A journey on the "Rossfeldhöhenring" Road (Rossfeld Panorama Road) leads you to an altitude of 1600 metres, high in the Alpine mountains of the Berchtesgadener Land. At the peak you will find a large car-park, here you can enjoy the stunning views to the huge massif of mountains like the Hohen Göll, Mount Kehlstein, the Trennen & Dachstein Mountains, Mount Untersberg as well as the beautiful Berchtesgadener Land and Salzburger Land. Two pretty mountain inns provide a good reason to stop and have some refreshments. The road is open throughout the year, however there is a small toll.

Without any doubts, Rossfeld is the most snow-reliable family skiing region (natural snow) in the Berchtesgadener Land. Four ski-lifts open up a well-kept ski-slope and a separated snowboard-piste with half pipe and leisure park. In the Rossfeld Ski-Hut with its large sun terrace, traditional Bavarian and local dishes are served. The connection to the Austrian skiing region Zinken-Bad-Dürrnberg opens unlimited skiing pleasure on more than 25 ski- and snowboard-pistes.

## Lakes

**Lake Königssee and St Bartholoma**

Ranked a German National Tourist Board "Top 100 Sights in Germany"

Surrounded by towering rocks and mountains, the emerald green Lake Königssee is Germany's cleanest lake. Since 1909 all the boats on the lake have been battery powered to preserve the cleanliness of the water. The lake is 8 kilometres long and on average is 150 metres deep. Various types of fish, such as trout, pike, perch and salmon, can be found in the lake. During the reign of the Bavarian Royal Family, 9 paddleboats operated on the lake, but today in summer, there are up to 18 sightseeing boats on the lake.

The trip to St Bartholoma takes just over one hour and unless the lake is frozen, can be taken at any time of the year. A popular part of the trip is to listen to the "echo" as the boatman sounds the trumpet.

Once at St Bartholoma, you can take a stroll along the shore, visit the small chapel or have a meal or snack in the small restaurant while waiting for a return boat. The Palace and pilgrimage church of St Bartholoma were founded by the Prince-Provosts of Berchtesgaden in 1134. The design of the church dates back to 1697; the stucco-work is by the Salzburg master Joseph Schmidt. In the 18th century the summer and hunting palace was rebuilt, incorporating the older building sections. In 1810, when Berchtesgaden became part of Bavaria, the palace became a hunting lodge for the Bavarian kings and was one of their favourite places. Over the centuries, the world-famous pilgrimage church, set against the Watzmann range, has been a source of inspiration for numerous landscape painters.

The boat trip is beautiful at any time of the year; lush green trees hug the mountains in spring and summer, rich gold's and reds in autumn and the bright white of the snow in winter all contrast with the blue green of the lake. In the summer months you can continue the boat trip further up the lake to Salet and then take a 15-minute walk to Lake Obersee, the second deepest lake in the area at a depth of 51 metres.
www.bayerische-seenschiffahrt.de

## Lake Hintersee

The lake was formed over 2000 years ago, but as the Klausbach stream brings down sand and gravel, slowly shrinking the lake in size. The area has always been very popular with writers and artists as well as walkers. The road along the lakefront has shops and cafes and was once the transportation route of the salt mined in Berchtesgaden. There are a few historic buildings of note; the Gasthof Auzinger is one of the oldest mountain inns in the area and was built in 1863 and opposite is the Altes Forsthaus, built in 1857 as the hunting lodge for Maximilian I. If you travel along the valley towards Hirschbichl, you can see the deer being fed in wintertime, daily around 3pm. Today the lake is popular for fishing and fresh fish caught in the lake are served in the cafes. Follow the pretty path around the lake or rent a paddle-boat or rowboat and glide across the glistening surface of this lake which has been used as a backdrop for many films. It is not possible to swim in the lake.

## Lake Höglwörth

This charming lake is a one of a kind with a romantic island castle, also worth seeing is the old abbey with its castle, church and cloister. A leisurely stroll around the lake will show off the location at its best. A secret tip is that swimming is made more enjoyable in Lake Höglwörth because of its pleasantly warm water.

## Lake Saalachsee

Lake Saalachsee was created by damming the Saalach River in Kibling. With the commissioning of the hydroelectric power plant in 1913, in particular for the electrification of the railway line from Salzburg, through Bad Reichenhall and on to Berchtesgaden, environmentally friendly hydroelectric power for Bad Reichenhall was possible. Here you can enjoy the beauty of nature by either cycling or walking upriver undisturbed and around this lovely lake.

## Lake Abtsdorfersee

Lake Abtsdorfersee near Laufen is definitely an ideal destination for families with its swimming beach, playground, free sunbathing area and swimmers will be happy to know that this is one of the warmest lakes in Bavaria.

## Lake Thumsee

Lake Thumsee located in a conservation area just outside of Bad Reichenhall, is a crystal-clear swimming lake with a lovely grassed area for sunbathers. Also charming, is the walking path that completely surrounds the lake, popular with walkers in summer and the when the lake freezes in winter it is just as popular with skaters and curling enthusiasts.

**Top Tip:**
Very close is the Seemösl, the outflow of Thumsee forms a marsh pond,

which is covered with hundreds of water lilies! It was created in 1936 and is considered by experts as the oldest of its kind in Germany.

## Lake Listsee

Lake Listsee by Bad Reichenhall is favourite for those who enjoy observing animals and nature. Not only are there large numbers of fish seen through the clear waters, but, for early risers, there is a chance of catching a glimpse of a stork catching its breakfast as well. The water and surrounding area are protected by the Environmental Protection Agency.

## **National Park**

"Berchtesgaden is the Yellowstone Park of the German Alps"
Heinrich Nöe, Writer
Ranked a German National Tourist Board "Top 100 Sights in Germany"

The Berchtesgaden National Park is one of the oldest protected areas in the Alps. It is a beautiful mountainous world, with craggy steep cliffs and high mountains, from the low-lying Königssee to the height of the mighty Watzmann. Created in 1978 by the Bavarian State "Berchtesgaden Alpine National Park", Germany's only Alpine National Park shows little human intervention. Since then, their aim has been to focus on nature protection, recreation and environmental education. The Berchtesgaden National Park is not a park enclosed with fences and is free to enter. The area can be explored on foot, by bike (on designated trails) or with local public transportation. The Park incorporates the 5 townships mentioned earlier and each has an information point.

You will not only get to see wild alpine species such as the mountain goat, marmot, eagle, but also, with a little bit of luck, the rare golden eagle. The flora and fauna reflects the diversity of the Berchtesgaden landscape. The flora is equally beautiful and includes, for example, the Hausmann's rock jasmine and the dwarf alpine rose.

The Jennerbahn is very popular among visitors, and will bring you up to the boundaries of the National Park at 1,800 metres. Up here, on hiking or mountain climbing trails, you can relax and enjoy the peace and beauty of the alpine landscape.

National Parks have always maintained the idea that they should be accessible to the public, and this one is no exception. Here there are over 200 kilometres of hiking trails that are well sign-posted, however in order to protect the Park it is important that visitors remain on the marked trails. During the summer months, overnight huts and mountain inns are open to hikers. In addition, many of the mountain pastures huts offer fresh dairy products in the National Park during the grazing period.

The hiking trails are split into 5 categories to suit all abilities:
**A Relaxed Pace** – easy walks with gentle inclines, less than 2 hours duration and possible refreshments along the way
**Short but Challenging** – a degree of fitness is required, some steep climbs, 2 to 3 hours duration and usually refreshments available at the peak
**Lengthy but Worth the Effort** – a degree of stamina is required as these last between 6 and 8 hours (round trip), along the valleys, you should have proper walking shoes and take water and snacks with you
**Heights** – recommended for experienced hikers, steep climbs into the mountains
**Trails for Wheelchairs and Children / Pushchairs** – there are several trails available for wheelchairs and pushchairs to enable everyone to enjoy the scenery

Organised hikes are available with a variety of themes including botany, geology, birdcalls, mountain forests, farming and simple nature walks.

For more information on the National Park www.nationalpark-berchtesgaden.de

## Things to See and Do

There are many things to do for all ages throughout the year in Berchtesgaden and its surrounds. I have divided the main attractions into 3 categories; all year round, summer and winter. However some of the attractions could be possible out of the normal season depending on the weather.

### Events throughout the Year

**January:**
6 – Festival of Three Kings, children dress up and go house to house singing

**February:**
Fasching carnival (dates vary each year) with the fancy dress finale on Shrove Tuesday
**Palm Sunday:**
Blessing of the palm bushes seen in fields, homes and cemeteries
**Pentecost (Whit Monday):**
Salt Miners Parade
**May:**
Spring Volksfest, a large tent is set up in Berchtesgaden with beer and live music
**June:**
Obersalzberg to Rossfeld old-timer car rally
24 - (St Johns Day) – lighting of bonfires at the top of mountains
26 – Annual church service at St John and Paul's chapel at St Bartholoma
**July:**
Schellenberger Dult – a traditional country fair
Second Sunday – Berchtesgaden folklore and shooters day
Last weekend – procession to Ettenberg church
**August:**
First weekend – celebrations and fireworks at Königssee
Last Saturday – pilgrimage to St Bartholoma church
**September:**
Almabetrieb – colourfully decorated animals return from mountain pastures
Autumn Volksfest - same as spring
**Advent:**
Christmas Markets
Christmas Eve – shooters can be heard in the afternoon
New Year's Eve – shooters between 11.30pm and midnight

# All Year Round

**Shopping and Local Souvenirs**

There are no major shopping centres for you to visit however each town offers you a selection of small independent shops with local products and souvenirs for sale. Here are a few of the products made locally:
Bad Reichenhall salt, this pure salt is taken from the local mines and is available for sale all over Germany.
Meindl Outdoor Shoes, these have been produced in the area for over 300

years and are of the highest quality having been improved and developed over the centuries. The quality can be assured as each shoe has a traceable identification number inside should there be the need to check production.

Chiba Gloves have been produced in Teisendorf for over 150 years and they have been the proud suppliers of outdoor sports gloves to the Austrian Imperial Family.

Beer souvenirs could include those from the Weininger Brewery in Teisendorf, the Bürgerbräu in Bad Reichenhall or the Hofbräuhaus in Berchtesgaden.

Grassl Schnapps is also a popular souvenir (more details later in chapter).

**Lake Königssee**

As detailed earlier, take a scenic boat trip on the lake in one of the many boats or a walk around the lake.

**Cable Car Rides**

**Top Tip:**
When considering a cable car ride it is always better to choose a bright, clear day in order to make the most of the views from the top.

**Jennerbahn Cable Car** (1,874m / 6,150ft)

Why not take a trip up Mount Jenner in a cable car, the highest gateway for visitors into the Berchtesgaden National Park.

Attractive two-person gondolas rise up from Schönau below into brilliant sunlight, over dark forests and rugged cliffs along the way. Soar up to a 1,802 metre high plateau, right in the middle of spectacular mountain landscapes to where the Bavarian poet Ludwig Ganghofer once said "He, whom God loves, is dropped into this Land!" No wonder, blessed with a panorama of more than 100 German and Austrian mountain peaks it is something quite special.

For those for whom simply admiring the view is not enough, over a dozen hiking trails with various levels of difficulty begin here and invite you to see some of the most beautiful areas in the Bavarian Alps. Hang-gliders and paragliders take off into the lofty heights and in winter skiers and snow boarders descend down the snowy mountain trails. Whether relaxing in a lounge chair at Germany's highest cafeteria or taking part in challenging and exciting sport. The Jenner Mountain can fulfil every wish, in summer as well as in winter.

**Predigtstuhl Cable Car (Predigtstuhlbahn)**

Take a ride in the oldest, large cabin cable car in the world still in its original condition. Built in 1928, this piece of nostalgia is right out of the past. Technically perfect in form, guests are pleasantly transported in around 8 minutes up to the top of Predigtstuhl Mountain at an elevation of

1,583m / 5,200ft). Admire the spectacular scenery en route as you journey up to the peak. Hiking trails which begin from the top will give you the opportunity of continuing on foot to the surrounding peaks or back to Berchtesgaden if you prefer. Great fun for the whole family!

**Obersalzberg Cable Car**

The mountains call and, thanks to the Obersalzberg cable car, your day out can be even more enjoyable. Without much effort, this is the way to take in the pure mountain air and enjoy the mountain scenery at your own pace. The Obersalzberg cable car gives access to a large number of hiking trails at the elevation of about 1,000 metres (3,300 ft.).

From here, the Documentation Centre at Obersalzberg and the Eagle's Nest bus departure point are about 2 km (1.2 miles) away. In the winter, equipped with a rental sled, the natural sledding track is a great way to swiftly reach the valley below and fun for the whole family.

**Chairlift at Hochschwarzeck (Hirscheckbahn)**

It is hard to believe how the perspective can change in just a few minutes. Glide up into the fresh mountain air on the Hirscheckbahn chairlift to take advantage of the hiking opportunities or just simply to enjoy the sun and the views.

In summer or winter the cosy inn on the mountain's high plateau is an inviting place for refreshments and a rest after a rewarding hike or a few ski runs. The panoramic view from the top is breath-taking; the peace and tranquillity remind you of times long gone in this day and age of noise and commotion. To rediscover nature at its best, a short ride on a chairlift might just make for a promising start!

**Documentation Obersalzberg**

9am to 5pm daily April to October
10am to 3pm November to March (closed Monday)
www.obersalzberg.de

The Documentation Centre on the Obersalzberg details the story of the town and the mountain during the reign of the Third Reich. There is a souvenir shop and restaurant at the car park/ bus stop and guides of the

Documentation can be bought at the Centre entrance. A public bus will take you to the Centre from Berchtesgaden.

**Salzbergwerk (Salt Mines)**

Bergwerkstrasse 83,
83471 Berchtesgaden
9am to 5pm 1st May to 15 October
11.30am to 3pm 16 October to 30 April
Special opening times operate during holidays and festivals.
www.salzbergwerk-berchtesgaden.de
Ranked a German National Tourist Board "Top 100 Sights in Germany"

Salt, known as "white gold", has been mined here since the 1517, when only a few people were allowed underground due to the value of the product. The mine produces around 160,000 tons of salt annually and at this rate the salt can be mined for another 300 years. Today anyone, young or old, can take this fascinating tour underground through the tunnels and caves.

First, you must don your special miners clothing, then on to a narrow railway followed by slides, which take you 650 metres into this secret world. Deep inside the mountain lights shimmer all around so as you glide across the sparkling lake on a raft in the Salt Grotto, which is dedicated to the fairy-tale King Ludwig II, you can see the full effect of this hidden marvel. The tour, which takes up to 2 hours, is very popular with families. Guided tours are available, as are souvenirs from the shop at the end.

**Alte Saline**

Alte Saline 9
Bad Reichenhall
www.alte-saline-bad-reichenhall.de

These beautiful salt works were built by Ludwig I in 1834 after a fire devastated the town. The works were named "the most beautiful salt works in the World" in 1846 and remain one of Bavaria's most important industrial monuments today. The works are fascinating both above and below ground and the focal point is the main pumping hall. Guided tours offer visitors an insight into the history of the town, the Saline itself and the importance of the White Gold, salt. Tours last around 1 hour. There is a souvenir shop next door.

**The Royal Castle**
Schlossplatz 2,
83471 Berchtesgaden
10am to 12pm & 2pm to 4pm Pentecost to October15th (closed Saturday)
11am and 2pm Monday to Friday October 16 to Pentecost (closed Saturday)
www.haus-bayern.com

Situated in central Berchtesgaden, this is the town's oldest building and was a monastery from the twelfth century until it came under the ownership of the Bavarian Royal Family in 1803. Although initially used as a summer residence, Crown Prince Rupprecht and his bride Crown Princess Marie Gabriele lived here for just over a decade in the early twentieth century. It was he who furnished the castle with most of the collections you can see here today, including an impressive collection of Nymphenburg porcelain. There are many fine exhibits of art, armour and more recently deer and hunting memorabilia.

## Schloss Adelsheim

Schroffenbergallee 6
83471 Berchtesgaden

The Schloss Adelsheim local heritage museum houses an extensive collection featuring local art and handicrafts such as typical Berchtesgaden wood and bone carvings, painted wooden boxes, colourful wooden toys, as well as furniture, weapons, household items and traditional clothing.

The museum's shop in Schlossplatz offers authentic Berchtesgaden-made handicrafts.

## Grassl Distillery

Salzburgerstrasse 105,
83471 Berchtesgaden
May to October: 8am to 6pm Monday to Friday, 8am to 2pm Saturday
November to April: 8am to 5pm Monday to Friday, 8am to Midday Saturday
www.grassl.com

The Grassl family has been distilling the gentian schnapps for over 400 years and this is the oldest schnapps distillery in Germany. The distillery and shop are situated on the main road to Salzburg just a few kilometres from Berchtesgaden. There is a huge variety of schnapps, liqueurs and fruit brandies available, as well as chocolates. You can also purchase souvenir glasses, hats, ceramics and local wooden gifts such as breadboards. Tours of the distillery are available followed by tasting of the schnapps and spirits.

The Grassl family could be regarded as an early "von Trapp" family. When the area was first in Bavarian rule, the family lost their right to distil schnapps, so they opened a small inn. They developed their musical talents in order to entertain their guests. Their reputation grew and soon they were performing throughout Europe. In 1842 the family was called to perform at the Royal Court in Munich. King Ludwig I was so impressed with their performance that afterwards he asked Franz Grassl if he had any special requests, so Franz explained how the family has lost the distilling rights. The King immediately gave the rights back to the Grassl family and the distillery continues to this day.

## Watzmann Therme

Bergwerkstrasse 54,
83471 Berchtesgaden
www.watzmann-therme.de

A paradise for swimmers of all ages whatever the weather, with indoor and outdoor pools, it is an adventure swimming world all under one roof. There are numerous pools, two of which are saltwater and a number of different activities including an 80-metre black hole slide. Saunas, massage and other fitness and wellness treatments are on offer. In the summer months there are deckchairs outside for you to soak up the sun. The outdoor areas also have beach volleyball courts and table tennis facilities. If all this makes you hungry, there are snacks and drinks available.

## Rupertus Therme

Friedrich-Ebert-Allee 21
Bad Reichenhall
www.rupertustherme.de

The Rupertus Therme is located in the most beautiful surroundings close to the mountains and parks. There are many facilities for all the family to enjoy pools, small children's pools, spa, saunas, solariums, fitness centres and much more. The Therme prides itself on the quality of the facilities and how it looks after all visitors. There are several cafes and restaurants for you to enjoy a relaxing coffee, drink or snack while you are here.

## Lokwelt

Westendstrasse 5
Freilassing
www.lokwelt.freilassing.de

This railway museum is an extension of the Deutsches Museum in Munich. Here you will find over 150 years of railway history. Located in an old railway depot on rail tracks between Munich and Salzburg the museum has attracted over 40,000 visitors since it's opening in 2006. For younger visitors (6 – 12 years) "Little Lokwelt" is focused on bringing the railway to life for them in a colourful and interactive way. New to the museum is the locomotive simulator where young and old can live out their dreams to be an engine driver.

# Summer

### Kehlsteinhaus "Eagle's Nest"

www.kehlsteinhaus.de
www.eagles-nest-tours.com

For details see earlier chapter on Berchtesgaden and the Third Reich

### Wimbachklamm
Near Ramsau

Over thousands of year the River Wimbach has been eroding the rock face in the Wimbach valley. The result is this awe inspiring gorge. The force of the water is so strong in places that water pools have been formed from the water pounding down from the rock walls into the riverbed.

Local foresters were the first to build a bridge through the gorge to help transport wood out of the valley. The wood was needed for the salt mines in Berchtesgaden.

They stopped removing wood for the mines in 1843 and the wooden bridge was opened to the public for the first time in 1847.

This path along the gorge allows walkers to be captivated by this fantastic work of nature.

**Almbach Gorge**

1$^{st}$ May - 31$^{st}$ October

The Almbach Gorge is accessible in both directions - to and from Ettenberg and to and from Maria Gern.

At the entrance of the Almbach Gorge you can see Germany's oldest marble ball mill. Since 1683 rough marble rocks have been ground to gleaming marbles by the force of the water.

Hiking through the gorge, which is of a distance of 3 kilometres, is beautiful in the summer months, with its waterfalls it is one of the most beautiful, wild romantic gorges of the Bavarian Alps, past your feet the crystal clear water cascades down to the valley.

A secure path leads you over bridges, stairs and tunnels through the impressive gorge with an altitude difference of about a 200 metres the upper section of the gorge broadens into a rolling valley. Follow the signs to the pilgrimage chapel of Ettenberg. Here you can look at the gorgeous frescos in the tiny chapel and perhaps enjoy a well-deserved rest at tavern Messnerwirt.

A steep hiking trail with lovely viewpoints leads you back to the marble mill. Hiking time is about two hours.

**Sommerrodelbahn**

Alpengasthof Hochlenzer
Scharitzkehlstrasse 6,
83471 Berchtesgaden
10am to 7pm daily May to October
www.hochlenzer.de

This is great entertainment for all the family high on the Obersalzberg. This specially built rodel (sledge) track stretches for 800 metres down the mountain. You sit in special sledges and off you go down the track with twists and turns along the way. You can also drive special carts similar to dodgems or try euro bungee, where you are attached to bungee type ropes and you bounce on trampolines.

If this is too energetic or you are tired from all this activity, there is a café that serves food and drink and has a children's play area to the side. The views of Berchtesgaden below are fantastic.

## Sports in and around Salzburg and Berchtesgaden

There are a great variety of sports available in Salzburg and the Bavarian Alps for visitors all year round.

## Summer

When the last snows of spring have melted the mountains take on their fresh green appearance and people want to enjoy the clean fresh air. Summer offers a huge range of outdoor sports, whether you are a novice or full of experience. There is no better way to appreciate the beauty of this area than getting out and about in the fresh mountain air and green hills.

**Jogging and Nordic walking** can be enjoyed along the banks of the Salzach. You can take clearly marked routes south towards Hellbrunn or north towards Oberndorf, either direction allows you to enjoy some beautiful scenery along the river and through parks.

### Hiking

For hikers there are the short walks up the city mountains in Salzburg such as the Mönschberg for a couple of hours or perhaps you prefer a longer hike, the Untersberg and the Gaisberg are not far from the city and have many clearly defined routes.

Hiking is the number one activity in the Berchtesgaden area and there are over 200 kilometres of well signposted trails in the area. These range from gentle strolls for all the family or mountain hikes that offer spectacular views. You can walk on your own or take a guided walk as part of a group. The guided walks include the Jenner, the mountain pastures around Königssee or a walk to the ice chapel at St Bartholoma. A walk that is challenging but still suitable for all the family is from the village of Maria Gern to the top of the Kneifelspitze. The walk takes about 2 hours, and from the top you can get great views along the valley and on a clear day you can see as far as Salzburg. There is a café at the top for refreshments and an alternative route back down that will take you to Berchtesgaden. For a gentle downhill walk, take the cable car from Berchtesgaden up the Obersalzberg and then follow the trail back down through the trees; this is the sledging path in winter. The trail is approximately 4.5 kilometres.

## Mount Untersberg

Lots of myths and tales revolve around the Untersberg Mountain. According to the various legends the mountain is home to earth spirits, fairies, magicians, witches and other creatures. It is said that Charlemagne is living inside the Untersberg with his knights. Every now and then the tired knights awake and a squire is sent out to count how many ravens are circling the mountain. If there are exactly 24 of them, the emperor will ride out with his knights and rescue Germany from great troubles... at least according to the legend.

A popular hike on the Untersberg is to the Toni-Lenz Hütte. From the car park near Markt Schellenberg, the wide trail leads through delightful old beech woods. Every now and then along the way you will see two lower ditches, the Bachgraben and the Lochgraben, with occasional pools and waterfalls. Halfway up you will leave the road to follow a small path, here the shade from the trees will lessen but the view will improve.

At the mountain hut you can enjoy refreshments, along with a beautiful view of the surrounding mountains from the terrace. The Toni-Lenz Hütte is also a popular destination with mountaineers as it serves as a base for extended hikes on the Untersberg.

Details of all walks, guided or not, can be found at the Tourist Offices

## Cycling

Another great way to get out and about is by bike. The area around Berchtesgaden has plenty of trails and quiet roads, from gentle scenic routes to more challenging off road trails on mountain bikes. You can cycle along the river to Königssee or take many of the quite roads around the village of Schönau. Bikes can be hired and details are at the Tourist Office.

Salzburg is known as the most bike friendly city in Austria. You can take cycling tours of the city or perhaps you want to tour the nearby countryside on your own, there is a vast cycle network that leads from the city to the countryside. Bikes can be rented in the city.

## Swimming

A family favourite is swimming and this is available both outdoors in summer and indoors all year round. There are 3 outdoor pools in Salzburg that open in May; Alpenstrasse, Volksgarten and Leopoldskron. The Paracelsus pool next to the Mirabell Gardens is open all year round and has other facilities such as saunas.

## Naturbad Aschauerweiher

Aschauerweiherstrasse 85
83485 Bischofsweisen
8.30am to 19.30pm May to October
(Weather permitting)

This is Germany's largest natural swimming pool and very popular with the locals on a warm day. Here you will find different pool areas set in beautiful parkland with the Bavarian Alps forming the backdrop. Filled with natural mountain water it is very good for those with skin allergies or irritations as there are no chemicals. Originally built in 1880 it was recently modernized in 2002. Today children can amuse themselves on the pirate island, the water slides and suspension bridge while adults relax on the wooden decking that surrounds the pools. Areas are set aside for beach volleyball and frisbee throwing. You can either take your own picnic or there is a restaurant for food and drink.

Other outdoor swimming pools near Berchtesgaden are:

## The Rupertus Therme

The Rupertus Therme is framed by the natural scenery of mountains, and benefits from the use of spring water and the mild alpine climate. The spa adjoins a vast park in Bad Reichenhall. The Spa & Family Resort Rupertus Therme is full of life and inner peace at the same time.

With unusual offerings such as sound and colour light pool, jacuzzi on the gallery, 850 square meters large sauna, health and fitness and many other more Rupertus Therme that meets the highest demands. Other facilities include: 120 metre tube slide, wave slides, and separate swimming area for small children, alpine garden and outdoor swimming, solarium, beauty centre and cafe.

## The Watzmann Therme

Dive into a paradise for the senses, which is surrounded by a gorgeous landscape! Experience in the Watzmann Therme a day full of fresh, sparkling pleasure and fun for all the family, indoors or out.

Feeling tense or in need of a pamper? Book a vitality and wellness day, treat yourself really well and recharge your strength and energy.

The attractive spa and water park has a water surface area of about 900 square metres. Facilities include: 80 metre Black Hole slide, outdoor pool and sun deck, separate area for small children, saunas, massage, waterfall, and restaurant.

## Schönau

The heated outdoor pool provides fun for all ages. The spacious green areas allow enough space for sunbathing and games. At over 900 square meters of water, the pool offers great fun and plenty of room for all as well as a water slide. There is also a snacks kiosk with guests' terrace.

## Outdoor pool Brodhausen Freilassing

The outdoor pool Freilassinger Brodhausen lies in an almost untouched landscape of meadows and trees. It offers: Float pool, slides a lazy river, climbing net, water bouncer, water cascades, floor jets, 2 children's pools, and playground.

## Adventure Park Badylon Freilassing

The Water Park Adventure Badylon has a separate non swimmer pool and a lap pool with a length of 25m. A 5m diving platform is also available. In the pool there is a slide, waterfall, massage jets, a steam room, a quiet gallery, a solarium and a separate baby-pool.

## Golf

Fancy a game of golf on Germany's highest course? The Gutshof on the Obersalzberg, at a height of 1000 metres, is a 9-hole course with spectacular views over the town below. This unusual course offers golf in the summer and skiing in the winter. The clubhouse was the Headquarters of the US military after the war.
There are 14 golf courses in and around Salzburg.

## Minigolf

If the full size game is not quite your thing, then a great family activity is minigolf. You can find courses at Luitpoldpark in Berchtesgaden and at Wimbachklamm in Ramsau.

Other organised sports that you can try in the area are mountain bike treks, river rafting, mountain treks, canyoning, archery and climbing.
For more information see www.asl-strub.de or www.outdoor-club.de

*As with all outdoor sports do not exceed your physical capabilities. Be prepared for all weathers and respect the landscape. If in doubt, check with the Tourist Office.*

# **Winter**

The Salzburgerland is a fantastic area for winter sports. Here you have over 2,200 kilometres of slopes in 110 resorts that are all easily accessible.

The Berchtesgadener Land really comes into its own in the winter when the snow has fallen. Even though the form of winter sports has changed over the years, the thrill and excitement associated with snow-covered mountains has remained the same.

Here in the Berchtesgadener Land you can experience a winter fairy tale setting. While the animals are hibernating under the ground, the winter sports are in full swing: skiing, sledding, ice-curling, ice-skating, cross-country skiing, bobsledding and cosy evenings in mountain huts.

Sledding or ice-curling is one of many traditional winter sport activities. Even a century ago Bavarian ice-curling or sledding parties were an integral part of winter here. If you prefer high speed, the ice-track at Königssee is just the thing for you. The first artificially refrigerated ice-track in the world, it is famed today as the venue for international bobsled or luge races. Whether as a spectator or a participant, the ice-track is a winter sports highlight.

## **Skiing**

For a day's skiing you can book the Salzburg Snow Shuttle either online before you travel or at the Tourist Office when you arrive. The Snow Shuttle costs less than 15 euros for the round trip and takes you to a different resort each day. The resorts are no more than an hour and a half away by coach. Ski passes and equipment hire can also be arranged, as well as information on the slopes. The coaches leave around 8am and are back in the city by 6pm. At the various resorts you can ski downhill, cross-country, try snowshoe walking or take a ride in a horse drawn sleigh.

The resorts visited include:
Flachau         www.flachau.at
Kitzbühel       www.kitzbuehel.com
Schladming      www.schladming-dachstein.at
Gastein         www.gastein.at
Zell am Zee     www.zellamzee.at

Cross Country skiing is available from around December to March (weather depending) on marked courses at Hellbrunn and Gaisberg.

The Bavarian Alps area became well known for its ski runs after the German Ski Championships were held here in 1934 and the fame continued when locals won medals at the Winter Olympics in nearby Garmisch-Partenkirchen in 1936. There are ski runs for all abilities and ski schools for beginners. Some of the more popular ski areas for downhill skiing are the Gutshof, Rossfeld, Götschen and the Jenner and with over 50 kilometres of runs there is plenty of choice.

It is also possible to do some cross-country skiing. The more popular areas for this are Schönau and at the Naturbad Aschauerweiher, which has a specially constructed track and five cross country routes for all abilities. There are over 90 kilometres of cross-country trails in the area.

## Sledging

If good old-fashioned sledging is your thing, then there are some fantastic natural tracks in the area. One of the most popular is on the Obersalzberg, where you can sled for over 4 kilometres down the hillside. The cable car in town will take you to the top. There are also sled runs at Bischofsweisen, Hintereck and Markt Schellenberg. This is extremely good fun for all the family, sledges can be hired at most sledge runs.

## Bobsleigh

The World Cup track at Königssee was constructed in 1968, was the first artificially frozen run, and hosts major World and European competitions every year. You can came and watch the competitions, usually free of charge, or in between times watch the German National teams train. When watching you get very close to the track. If you want to have a try yourself then you can take a ride, at over 100 km per hour, with a champion driver at the helm.
For Bobsleigh rides or competition dates
www.rennbob-taxi.de

## Ice Skating

Ice-skating is very popular with all the family and in winter you will find open-air rinks as well as indoor facilities. The most popular place to skate is on the Naturbad Aschauerweiher. You can also try Eisstockschiessen, which is a form of curling. Ice-skating in Salzburg is available in Mozartplatz and Volksgarten.

## Horse and Sleigh Rides

For something altogether more relaxing, take a horse and sleigh ride to the deer feeding station at Hirschbichl. Should the track not have enough snow then a cart will be used instead.

## Snow Shoe Walking

If you want to appreciate the scenery at a more leisurely pace and at close hand then perhaps snow shoe walking is for you. Organised walks are available in Berchtesgaden, Bischofsweisen, Schönau and Ramsau. Alternatively, you may want to have a walk at night by torchlight over the glistening pastures.

Details of which ski runs are open, ice rinks and other sports such as Nordic Walking and Snowboarding can be found at the Tourist Office. Equipment hire can also be arranged at the Tourist Office, www.berchtesgadener-land.com

Other places to arrange winter sports are www.asl-strub.de and www.outdoor-club.de

For lift and ski pass prices for the Jenner check www.jennerbahn.de

Berchtesgaden Ski School
Equipment hire, lessons in either a group or one to one.
www.skischule-berchtesgaden.de

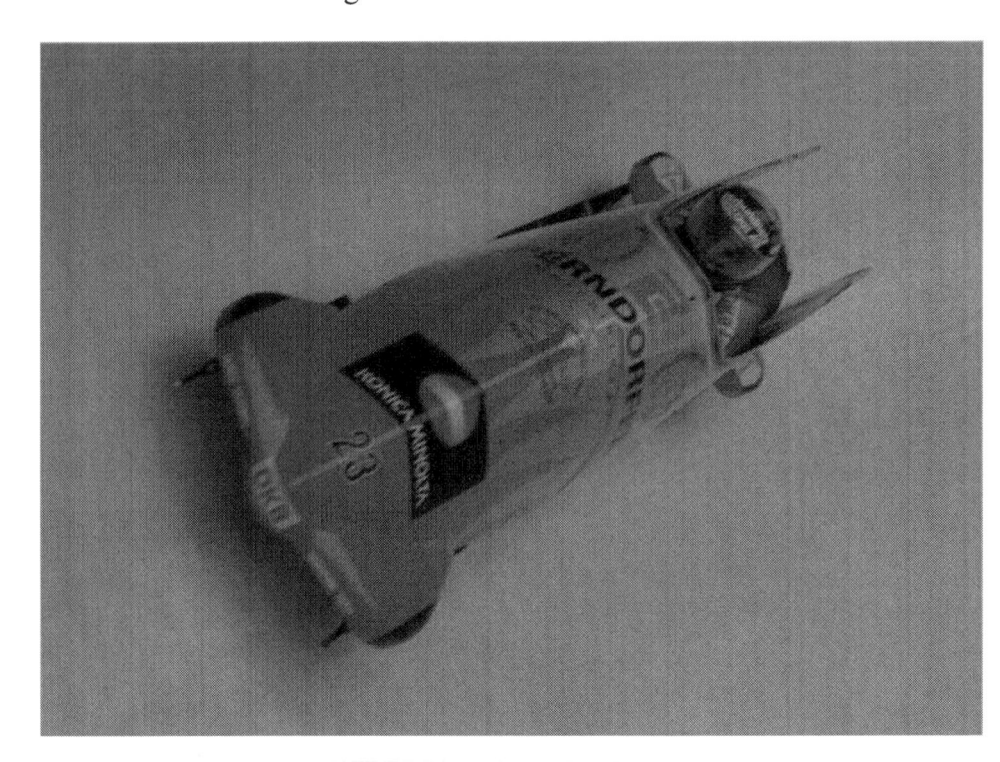

## **Advent in Berchtesgaden**

The Christmas and Advent season in Germany is a truly magical experience and Berchtesgaden is no exception. The narrow streets are lit with festive lights and the narrow streets and painted facades only add to the atmosphere. The shops stock Christmas goodies such as decorations and foods such as Stollen and the smell of warming Glühwein fills the air in restaurants and cafes.

The Christmas market stretches around the pedestrian area of Berchtesgaden and into Schlossplatz. Here the wooden huts sell ornaments of all descriptions, hats and gloves, foods and centuries old arts and crafts. You can take a torch lantern guide of the historic market town with the Night Watchman every Friday at 5pm from Schlossplatz. For children there is a painting workshop and also a children's bakery where they can make cookies to take home. In Schlossplatz there is a maze made from 250 Christmas trees. The nativity is performed every day and features live animals. The local blacksmith demonstrates his trade and produces metal gifts for visitors to buy. Horse and carriage rides are a lovely way to sample the atmosphere and leave every day from Nonntal between 2pm and 5pm. There is a musical programme which includes trumpets from the church tower every weekend at 2.30pm.

## Walking Tour of Berchtesgaden

This walk will show the highlights of the town centre.

**Königliche Villa (Royal Villa)**
Kälbersteinstrasse
www.fewo-lindenau.de

Maximilian II built the Royal Villa in 1850 in the classic Italian style. Many of the family members spent time here, but especially Ludwig II and his brother Otto. The façade features wood carved portraits of Maximilian and his wife Marie. The Villa is located opposite Luitpold Park and today is holiday accommodation. Proceed along Maximilianstrasse.

**Hotel Watzmann**
Franziskanerplatz 2
www.hotel-watzmann.com

The hotel was built in 1850 as a brewery but now houses one of the oldest hotels in Berchtesgaden. The restaurant is indoors but highly recommended is cake or ice cream on the outdoor terrace, from where you get great views of the Watzmann, the Jenner and the Kehlstein mountains.

**National Park Information Centre**
Franziskanerplatz 8
www.nationalpark-berchtesgaden.bayern.de

The building was originally built in 1401 as an Augustine convent but then became a Franciscan Monastery in the late 1600's. Franciscan monks still live in part of the building today. The centre offers information on the National Park including walks and hikes for all abilities including the disabled. Much of the material is available in English.
Toilets here are clean and free.

**Franciscan Church**
Franziskanerplatz

Adjoining the Nationalparkhaus is the Franciscan Church, built in 1480 in the gothic style. The church is known for the statue of the Madonna, the "ährenkleidmadonna", which translates as "Madonna wearing a dress of wheat heads". It is said to be a copy of a statue in Milan and has been an object of reverence since the 1600's.
The area that runs along behind these buildings is the Sonnenstrasse, and here you get good views of the town below and the surrounding mountains.

## Alter Friedhof (Old Cemetery)

To the side of the Franciscan Church is the oldest cemetery in Berchtesgaden and it came into existence in 1685. The graves are well looked after by family members and you will see that often a great number of people use the same grave, at different levels. There are a number of wall plaques representing those who died in the world wars, many in Russia. You will see at the end of the pathway a large stone with the name "Dietrich Eckart", he was known as the father of the Nazi party and Hitler's mentor.

## Kur and Kongress House

If you leave the cemetery at the north end, you will see the concrete building that is the Convention Centre. There are several rooms that can house meetings but it is often used for tourist talks and events, the restaurant regularly offers live music and dinner.

## Kurpark

Just past the Kur and Kongress House is the Kurgarten. This was originally the garden for the Royal Palace but today it is a quiet area of parkland for locals and visitors to relax in.

Occasionally in the summer you can listen to classical concerts in the park. On the left of the gate when you enter is a wooden sculpture depicting the "Christmas Shooters", a tradition that welcomes in Christmas and the New Year.

**Decorative Buildings**

From the Kurpark, cross over the road to the Metzgerstrasse and Marktplatz area. Here you can see many buildings decorated in the Lüftlmalerei style that is typical of the area.

**Pedestrian Area**

The centre of Berchtesgaden is now pedestrianised. Here you can walk around the shops or stop and enjoy a coffee and cake and watch the world go by. If you stand with Café Forstner in front of you, look up the hill to the left and you will see the Calvary, erected in 1760. You will see an eye set in a triangle and this marks the last stop in a trail that marks the four Stations of the Cross.

## Kaserer Haus

Not far from the Bier Adam restaurant, you will notice a donkey well. The donkey represents a German fairy-tale donkey, which produced gold. Behind you is the façade of the Kaserer Haus, which depicts the rebuilding of the town after much of it was destroyed by fire in the early 1600's. The Historical Society of Berchtesgaden protects this façade, along with many others.

## Marktplatz

The Marktplatz is part of the pedestrianised area and the focal point is the fountain. The fountain was first built in 1558 but has been remodelled several times since. The Bavarian symbol of a lion is the main feature of the fountain.

## Schlossplatz (Castle Square)

Through the archway from the Marktplatz and you find yourself in the cobbled Schlossplatz. If you look along the wall on your left you will see the war memorial for the locals killed in the Second World War, and the Royal Castle is on your right. At the far end of the square is the Stiftskirche, built in the twelfth century by the Augustine monks. The square is the setting for a Christmas market in December.

## Stiftskirche (Collegiate Church)

The Augustine monks built this twelfth century church. The interior boasts a thirteenth century chancel, Gothic choir stalls from 1440 and a high altar from 1669.
Leaving the square through the arch next to the Stiftskirche brings you to Nonntal, the oldest street in Berchtesgaden.

# **Walking Tour of Bad Reichenhall**

There is a lot to see in the town of Bad Reichenhall, old buildings, historic churches and many fountains. This tour begins and ends at Rathausplatz.

## Rathausplatz

The Altes Rathaus was built by architect Lucas in 1849, the frescoes were a later addition in 1924. These frescoes show from left to right, Charlemagne, St Rupert, Emperor Frederick I and King Ludwig I and they are accompanied by Charity and Justice. Across from the Altes Rathaus is the Neues Rathaus. The Wittlesbach fountain was added to the centre of the square in 1905. Another fountain in Rathausplatz is the Dreieck Trinkbrunnen.

From here cross over to the

**Alte Saline and Salzmuseum**

For thousands of years the livelihood of the residents of Bad Reichenhall depended upon salt. After a devastating fire destroyed the medieval salt works in 1834, Ludwig I commissioned these works to be built. Across from the Alte Saline stands the former salt refinery administration building. Constructed in the neo classical style in 1839, the building is an important architectural monument.

There are several fountains to be seen in this area; the AlpenSole Brunnen, the St Rupertusbrunnen and the St Virgiliusbrunnen.

Turn left along Salinenstrasse

**St Nikolaus Kirche**

Parts of the church of St Nicholas have been destroyed on several occasions and subsequently rebuilt. The 1862 frescoes above the altar show the Holy Trinity and 4 patron saints: St George, St Nicholas, St Corbinian and St Pancras. These frescoes and the Stations of the Cross in the side naves are the only surviving works of the artist Moritz von Schwind.

Cross over

**Floriansviertel (Upper Town)**

Florianiplatz is a typical Alpine square with many gabled houses. In the centre of Florianiplatz is the Floriani fountain. This neighbourhood is one of the towns oldest and has many preserved house facades and the medieval town defence walls from the 13$^{th}$ century. The towers named after St Peter and St Paul is one of 14 ancient fortified towers from the town.

## Burg Gruttenstein

The medieval fortress still maintains the 3-storey high Gothic central building. To the south the Pulverturm (Powder Tower) rises up from the ancient city walls.

Head back towards the town centre to the right of Alte Saline

## Ludwigstrasse

This forms the central pedestrian area of the town and the main shopping area. The Wisbacher fountain is on the corner of Ludwigstrasse and Wisbacherstrasse. Other fountains to see in the pedestrian area of Ludwigstrasse are the Drei Tanzen Mädchen, Zwei-Buben-Brunnen and the Mozart-Brunnen.

Carry along and then on to Salzburgerstrasse, you will pass the Stork Fountain, the Stadtbach and the Füllhornbrunnen, all on Salzburgerstrasse.

## Stift and Stiftskirche St Zeno

The church with its 3 nave basilica dates back to the 12$^{th}$ century. Among the highlights are the Romanesque doorway and the Lord's Prayer written in ancient German in the vestibule. In the Baroque wing of the monastery is a Romanesque cloister. There are 2 fountains here, the Heiliger St Zeno fountain in front of the church and the Entenbrunnen close by.

Head back towards town and on your left

## Kurpark

The Kurpark was laid out in 1870 and the Kurhaus was added later in 1900. In 1910 the court architect, Drolinger, added the impressive open air inhalatorium (Gradierwerk) and in 1912 he built the Wandelhalle with its concert rotunda which can seat 500 people for concerts. The Kurmittelhaus was built in 1928 in the late Jugendstil style. The modern Kurhaus was opened in 1988.

There are several fountains to see in the park, the Alpen-Sole fountain is in front of the Gradierwerk, the Kaiser-Karl Alpen - Sole fountain at the Wandelhalle and Wassertretbecken in front of the Kurmittelhaus.

Continue along Kurstrasse, the Star Fountain is on this street

## Evangelische Kirche

This neo gothic Evangelical church was built in 1881, and the Bismarck fountain is located in front of the church.

Walk along Bahnhofstrasse, you will see the Salzsäule Fountain outside number 21 and the Hallosbrunnen outside number 22.

## St Johannes Spitalkirche

First documented in 1144, this is the oldest church in Bad Reichenhall. The Romanesque church arches and Gothic choir organ have been preserved, however the interior of the church was redesigned in the late 18$^{th}$ century.
Adjacent the church, the old city wall joins the Salzburg Gate.

Continue along the same road

## Poststrasse Pedestrian Zone

This pedestrian zone was laid out in 1992 in the centre of the historical part of town. The newly rediscovered sections of the original town stream were integrated into the new town stream.

The following are all in the pedestrian area heading back towards Rathausplatz.

## Salzmaierhaus

A marble statue in front of the building depicts the Salzamtschreiber and clearly demonstrates that this was the Salt Works Administration building until 1840. The Stadtbach mit Quellstein und Fontänenbrunnen is on Poststrasse in front of the Salzmaierhaus.

**Local Heritage Museum**

This building was used to store extra grain in times of need but now houses the Local Heritage Museum.

**Agidplatz**

Centuries ago the Archbishops subjects lived here and the square has maintained its character and appearance ever since. The square is surrounded by the old fire station that now houses an adult education centre, a small theatre, a gallery and a music school.

**St Agid Kirche**

First built in 1159 in the Romanesque style the church of St Agid was later rebuilt in the 15$^{th}$ century in the Gothic style.

The St Agid Wandbrunnen and the Friedenstaube-Brunnen are situated in and around the church and square.

## Where to Eat and Drink in Berchtesgaden

I have already detailed in a previous chapter the type of food you can expect to get ion the area, here are some of our favourite places to eat around Berchtesgaden area.

Please note that I have stated if there are guest rooms available however this is purely for your information and does not indicate the standards of accommodation.

**Café Forstner**
Open daily 9am to 6pm, Sundays and holidays 10am to 6pm

Located in the pedestrianised centre of Berchtesgaden, this café is ideal for a mid-morning or afternoon coffee and cake. The cakes are homemade and there is a vast selection from fruit tortes to chocolate cake. Indoor seating is available upstairs and in summer tables are available outdoors, where you can may want to opt for homemade ice cream. The café also has a small shop where you can buy cake to takeaway or perhaps a gift or souvenir of chocolates or pralines.
www.cafe-forstner.de

## Café Lockstein

Just a short, but fairly steep walk up from the centre of Berchtesgaden, is Café Lockstein. From the terrace you get good views over the town centre. This is a good place for coffee and cake or a lunchtime snack. Self-catering apartments are also available for rent.
www.cafe-lockstein.de

## Gasthaus Bier Adam
Open daily from 9am to Midnight
www.bier-adam.de

Centrally located, this traditional restaurant is the oldest in Berchtesgaden and first opened over 400 years ago. The kitchen serves delicious home cooked food. Rooms are to both sides of the entrance and in warmer weather there are a couple of tables set outside. The Gasthaus is highly decorated with the fresco painting on the outside walls.

## Hubertus Stüben

This traditional Stübe is part of the Hotel Vier Jahreszeiten, which is located on Maximilianstrasse. It is small and cosy with the tables being arranged over 2 levels. Traditional paintings and decorations such as antlers adorn the walls and the food is delicious. The hotel and restaurant have been in the same family for many years and they take great pride in the standards they keep. I have not stayed in the hotel but would definitely consider it because of its close proximity to the town centre.
www.hotel-vierjahreszeiten-berchtesgaden.de

## Gasthof Goldener Bär
Food served daily from 9am to 10pm
www.gasthof-goldener-baer.de

This is one of our favourites, situated in the pedestrian area. The restaurant has been under the same family ownership since 1883 and the owners are very much in presence, which ensures a high standard of food and service. Downstairs is a small room with an assortment of large wooden tables and smaller booth tables. When busy, the upstairs room is used; this is a large high-ceilinged room with a variety of tables. Personal recommendations are steak, goulash or schnitzel. You can also have breakfast here from about 4 euros. In the summer there are a few tables outside.

## Hofbräuhaus Berchtesgaden
www.hofbrauhaus-berchtesgaden.de

Just a few minutes' walk from the town centre on Bräuhausstrasse; the brewery is a popular place with locals and tourists alike. When you first enter you should turn to the right, there you will see the food counter with the steaks and pork knuckles ready to be served. The first few tables are primarily for drinkers but as you carry on through the room becomes more of a restaurant. The beer is their own, naturally, and the atmosphere warm and welcoming. The menu also offers daily specials. At busy times there is a large function room to the left of the front door and that is opened up as extra seating.

## Hotel Edelweiss
Maximilianstrasse 2

This recently built hotel offers good quality accommodation as well as a choice of places to eat. There is an a la carte restaurant, the Weinstübe with a good choice of wines and spirits or alternatively an informal restaurant offering not only Bavarian dishes and snacks but also pizza and pastas.

# Schönau

There are several cafes and restaurants in Schönau, particularly if you want something to eat when you spend the day around the lake. I can particularly recommend the Alter Bahnhof and the Seeklause.

**Alter Bahnhof**
Seestrasse 17
Schönau am Königssee
www.alter-bahnhof-koenigssee.de

Alter Bahnhof is located close to the car park on the left hand side as you make your way towards the lake and the shops. It has a series of small rooms depending on how busy they are or tables outside in the summer. They make delicious soups and serve fish fresh from the lake as well as pork and meat dishes. There is a children's menu available.

**Seeklause**
Seestrasse 6
Schönau am Königssee
www.koenigsseer-hof.de

The Seeklause is close to the bus stop from town and on the right hand side of the main entrance. Inside it is traditionally set out with wooden tables and chairs and on the way to the toilets you can see a small collection of vintage Bobsleigh. You can have coffee and cake for less than 5 euros, snacks such as soups or salads at a reasonable price and for main meals fish fresh from the lake as well as other Bavarian favourites. Guest rooms available.

**Gasthaus Unterstein**
Untersteinerstrasse
Schönau am Königssee
www.gasthaus-unterstein.de

There is a large restaurant inside and a lovely large beer garden outside for summer days. The menu offers Bavarian specialties as well as many seasonal events and specials.

**Echostuberl**
Seeklause 41
Schönau am Königssee
www.echostueberl.de

Located at the water's edge of the lake this restaurant offers good food with great views. The menu naturally offers a great number of fish dishes however Bavarian favourites such as steak, goulash and schnitzel are all available and perhaps you could have the chocolate fondue for 2 afterwards? For snacks and light meals during the day salads and soups are available as well as homemade cakes. In the summer, the outdoor terrace is popular and can sit up to 200 guests.

## Ramsau

**Gasthof Auzinger**
Hirschbichlstrasse 8
Ramsau
www.auzinger.de

This restaurant, located just a few minutes' walk from Lake Hintersee, has traditional wooden tables and chairs and painted scenes on the walls. The menu contains all the usual Bavarian specialties for lunchtime and evenings and in the afternoon there are warm and cold snacks as well as homemade cakes and tortes. There is a lovely beer garden and terrace in the summer with great views of the lake. Guest rooms are available.

**Tavern Wachterl**
Alpenstrasse 159
Ramsau
www.wirtshaus-wachterl.de

This small restaurant has a warm and friendly ambience inside and great views from the terrace in summer. They pride themselves on their food and have won awards for the cuisine. The philosophy is for good quality food, fresh from local suppliers and fresh seasonal produce and they certainly manage to achieve this.

## Gasthof Oberwirt
Im Tal 86
Ramsau
www.oberwirt-ramsau.de

Located between Königssee and Hintersee this restaurant has been here for over 500 years and is close to the famous church of St Sebastian. The small restaurant offers as specialties on its menu Schweinhaxe, Ox, beef and pork as well as homemade strudel for dessert. Guest rooms are available.

## Wörndlshof
Am See 21
Ramsau
www.woerndlhof.de

Located right on the water's edge this restaurant has great views of the lake. With a silver medal for its Bavarian cuisine all the traditional favourites are included on the menu as well as homemade cakes for afternoon snacks. There has been an inn on this site since 1461 and has been in the ownership of the current family for over 60 years. There is a lovely beer garden for the summer months and guest rooms are available too.

## In Other Local Towns

## Brennerbräu
Hauptstrasse 46
Bischofsweisen
www.brennerbraeu.de

This restaurant seats 260 guests and has been here since 1823. The interior features the traditional wooden tables and chairs as well as wooden ceilings and outside there is a sunny beer garden in summer. The menu includes white sausage breakfast, Schweinhaxe, and beer garden specialties such as Hendl, spare ribs and Steckerlfisch.

## Hofwirt
Salzburgerstrasse 21
Bad Reichenhall
www.hofwirt.de

This restaurant is located in the heart of historic Bad Reichenhall just minutes from the pedestrianised area and the train station. The Alpine restaurant has won many awards for its traditional cooking and there is also a heated garden restaurant. In summer there is a beer garden set amongst the fruit trees and a children's play area. Guest rooms available.

**Schwabenbräu**
Salzburgerstrasse 22
Bad Reichenhall
www.wieninger-schwabenbraeu.de

Centrally located with a traditional restaurant and a fantastic shady beer garden in the summer. There is an extensive menu with Bavarian specialties, pastas, daily specials and a children's menu. The beer is served fresh from the barrel and there is a good selection of wine and schnapps. Guest rooms available.

**Lohmayr Stubn**
Salzburgerstrasse 13
Piding
www.lohmayr.com

This family run Wirtshaus has a traditional menu with favourites such as Schnitzel and goulash but also has influences from Austria, France and the Far East to offer a great choice for the diner. There are seasonal menus and specials available. The family also offers accommodation in a holiday rental.

**Tollhouse**
Weissbach an der Alpenstrasse
Schneizlreuth
www.hotel-mauthaeusl.de

Situated in a beautiful location overlooking the mountains between Berchtesgaden and Bad Reichenhall this restaurant offers typical Bavarian specialties after 5pm in the evening. For daytime visitors the cafe is open for homemade cakes, tortes and strudels. In the summer there are 2 sun terraces offering outstanding views. There are also rooms and apartments for rent and a small spa.

# German Alpine Road

The German Alpine Road (Deutsche Alpenstrasse) was created in 1927, although the idea of linking Alpine villages along a route can be traced back to the mid nineteenth century, mainly for trade reasons at that time. The road is 450 kilometres in length, starts at Lake Constance (Bodensee) and ends at Königssee, taking in some breath-taking scenery. It is one of the longest established tourist routes in Germany and as you travel along you will see meadows, hills, mountains, forests, valleys and lakes as well as picturesque villages. The route leads past 25 castles, 21 mountain lakes and 64 spa towns and in summer you can make the most of the scenery by using one of the many cycle tracks, hiking trails or cable cars. Or perhaps in winter you would like to ski down some of the mountains along the way.

The route starts on Lake Constance in **Lindau (1)** and is the only town on the lake that is officially in Bavaria. Founded as a fishing town in Roman times and granted the status of a city in the 13$^{th}$ century. The old town stands on an island in the lake and is connected to the mainland by a road and railway bridge. The town still retains its medieval layout, centred on 3 main streets of gabled buildings.

Next is **Oberstaufen (2)**, a pretty little town in the western Allgäu. Here you can take the cable car to the top of the Hochgrat, the highest mountain in this area at a height of just over 1800 metres.

Continue along the route and you come to the town of **Füssen (3)**. In Roman times this town was sat on the road that linked northern Italy and the city of Augsburg. In 1313 the town came under the rule of the bishops of Augsburg who came here for the summer months. The next period of prosperity was in 1803 when Füssen became part of Bavaria and the Royal Family took an interest in the area, building the castles of Hohenschwangau and Neuschwanstein.

**Schloss Neuschwanstein (4)** is probably the most famous of Ludwig II castles, although he never got to see it completed. The castle has an enviable position sat on top of a rocky crag and you can get good views from the Marienbrücke, which spans the adjacent ravine. This castle was the model for Disney's Cinderella castle.

Just below Neuschwanstein is the yellow stoned castle of **Hohenschwangau,** where Ludwig II spent most of his childhood.
A few miles further along is another of Ludwig's castles, **Linderhof.** This is the smallest of the castles and the one he visited most often. The interior is in the French baroque style and the Hall of Mirrors is extravagantly decorated. The castle is surrounded by park and is popular with visitors.

Nearby are the small towns of **Ettal (6)** and **Oberammergau (5).** The Benedictine Monastery in Ettal is an impressive sight and attracts many pilgrims. The village of Oberammergau is a typical Bavarian village, with fresco painted buildings. It is best known for the Passion plays which are held every 10 years and are to thank God for saving the village from plagues and wars. You can buy beautiful woodcarvings here, including Christmas decorations as well as household goods. This town is the largest centre for wood carving in Germany.

The road continues and you then reach **Garmisch-Partenkirchen (7)**.
Originally 2 villages they combined to host the 1936 Winter Olympic Games and have remained so since. The centre of the village has many attractive buildings, shops and cafes. A popular shop is Kathe Wohlfahrt, a Christmas shop that is open all year round. At the edge of the town you can take the cable car to the top of the Zügspitze, Germany's highest mountain. If it is a clear day you will be able to see 4 countries from the

summit. The area is a popular ski resort in the winter.

From here the route enters what many consider to be the most scenic. You will pass through the holiday resort of **Benediktbeuren (8)** and its monastery.

You will find the town of **Bad Tölz (9)** with its pretty market square. The town is a health spa when iodine springs were discovered in 1946, and the water park that was built as a result is one of the largest in Germany. There is a very good local heritage museum.

Next on the road is the lake of **Tegernsee**. The 5 townships on the lakefront offer a typical view of Alpine life. You can take a boat around the lake or in summer hire rowing boats and see the sights under your own steam. From **Rottach-Egern (9)** you can take a cable car to the top of Wallberg and see the views from over 1700 metres.

In **Tegernsee (10)** itself, is the monastery and it's brewery. This town is the centre of activity around the lake and in summer is bustling with visitors. The area offers a lot of winter sports and walking and cycling opportunities in summer.

Not far from Tegernsee is **Schliersee (11)**, often considered the younger sibling. It offers a more peaceful setting and in summer the lakeside properties have flower-laden balconies.

The road winds its way along to **Bayrischzell (12)**, a traditional Bavarian village and health resort. In 1883 the first Alpine folklore association was founded here and you will usually see the residents in the local Bavarian dress.

The route now heads for **Chiemsee.** On an island in the lake is another of Ludwig's castles, **Herrenchiemsee (13)**, considered to be the Versailles of Bavaria. The castle is set in a park filled with statues, fountains and a canal. You take the boat from Prien to the island.

You are now on the final part of the route and heading down to **Ramsau (15) Berchtesgaden (16)** and Königssee. You will pass **Bad Reichenhall (14)**, famous for its salt and the resulting spa. The town has lovely parks, grand hotels and a pedestrianised centre.

An addition to the Alpine Road is the Rossfeld Panorama Strasse. This begins on the Obersalzberg and continues in a loop for 16 kilometres along the Rossfeld crest that separates Bavaria from Austria. You get breath-taking views and great skiing in winter.
www.deutsche-alpenstrasse.de
www.rossfeldpanoramastrasse.de

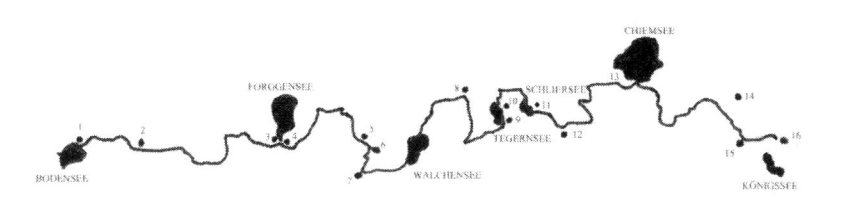

1 - LINDAU                7 - GARMISCH-PARTENKIRCHEN   13 - HERRENCHIEMSEE
2 - OBERSTAUFEN           8 - BENEDIKTBEUREN           14 - BAD REICHENHALL
3 - FÜSSEN                9 - BAD TÖLZ                 15 - RAMSAU
4 - NEUSCHWANSTEIN       10 - TERGERNSEE               16 - BERCHTESGADEN
5 - OBERAMMERGAU         11 - SCHLIERSEE
6 - ETTAL                12 - BAYRISCHZELL

## **Sleep**

There is a good selection of accommodation in both Salzburg and the Berchtesgaden area, from self-catering apartments, small family run hotels to 5 star luxury hotels, so there is something to offer every budget. You can find accommodation using one of the search websites or alternatively through the Tourist Office website. This can be a good option as I know from personal experience that they often have a number of rooms reserved at certain hotels that you can book at the same price, but the hotel website itself indicates there are no rooms available. There is a youth hostel set in parkland about 20 minutes' walk from Berchtesgaden. There are also camping sites in the area in Berchtesgaden and Schönau. Details of all of these can also be found on the Tourist Office website.

Hotels were first opened in Salzburg in the nineteenth century as tourism first began to draw the crowds to the city. There is a great variety of accommodation to choose from with prices to suit all budgets, from hostels up to 5 star luxury hotels. If you choose to stay in the old town you may pay a premium for location but in my view it is worth it. Salzburg has over 90 hotels in and around the city as well as over 30 privately owned bed and breakfast lodgings, 10 youth hostels, over 60 privately let apartments and 3 camping sites. Details of many can be sought from the tourist information offices.

# Get Around

The best way to get around Salzburg is by public transport. It is easy to find which way you are going as most buses and trolley buses head to the city centre (Centrum). The trolley buses operate every 10 minutes. Pre purchased tickets are the best value and they can be found at most tobacconists. A 24-hour ticket is valid for all buses within the city centre. If you are in Salzburg for more than 3 days then the best value is a weekly ticket (Wochenkarte). Children between the ages of 6 and 14 travel at reduced rates.

You must validate your ticket when you take your first ride on the bus or trolley bus.

Car rental is available both at the train station and the airport if you want to travel further afield.

## By Bus

There are regular buses that operate around Berchtesgaden taking you to Königssee, the Obersalzberg or other local towns such as Ramsau and Markt Schellenberg. The local buses will also take you to Salzburg. In Salzburg the local bus services will connect you with other local towns or perhaps take a trip to Munich on a national coach company such as Flixbus.

## By Train

If you are going to explore further afield in Bavaria e.g. Munich, then a Länder ticket will probably be the best option for you. This allows up to 5 people to have unlimited travel anywhere in Bavaria at a very reasonable price. Two children under the age of 14 count as one adult, so this is great for families. The train is also a good way to connect Salzburg with local towns, faster than the bus and a perfect way to enjoy the local scenery.

## By Taxi

There are several taxis in Berchtesgaden and you usually do not have to wait very long. I would recommend Taxi Angerer, a family operated company, who are very friendly and speak reasonable English. They also operate a shuttle service between Salzburg or Munich airport. For a shuttle quotation contact: info@taxi-angerer.de

Taxis operate in Salzburg and can be found outside most hotels.

## Car Hire

If you plan on seeing a lot of the area, then maybe hiring a car would be a good option. Car hire is available at both Munich and Salzburg airports and train stations. You can hire cars in Berchtesgaden, but I would recommend booking in advance as the garages are fairly small and do not have a large number of vehicles.

## Getting to Salzburg and Berchtesgaden

### By Car

Two major roads connect Berchtesgaden with other major cities. The A8 runs from Munich to Innsbruck and allows easy access from either city; Munich is a distance of 180 kilometres and Innsbruck 190 kilometres. The A1 runs from Vienna, through Salzburg to Berchtesgaden. Salzburg is only 20 kilometres.

All motor vehicles using motorways and expressways in Austria must have a toll sticker (Vignette). The cost of the toll depends on the size of the vehicle. They are available from petrol stations, tollbooths and some tobacconists.
The A8 goes to Salzburg from Munich, the A1 from Vienna and the E60 from Innsbruck.

### By Train

You can take the train from Munich, Vienna, Innsbruck to Berchtesgaden and this is a very relaxing way to travel, allowing you to see some of the Bavarian countryside and villages en route.
To check the latest train times and prices see www.bahn.de and the website is available in English. There are many offers available; therefore I recommend you check what is best for you.

You can take the train from Munich, Vienna and Innsbruck to Salzburg and this is a very relaxing way to travel, allowing you to see some of the countryside and villages en route.
To check the latest train times and prices the website, www.oebb.at which is available in English. There are many offers available; therefore I recommend you check what is best for you.
Salzburg main train station is important as a border station serving both Austria and Germany. It is served by Eurocity, Intercity and ICE trains from most European cities. For local travel, suburban trains go to most towns making visiting in the area convenient and easy. The station is a 15-minute walk from the old town; alternatively taxis are available at the

front entrance.

## By Plane

Munich airport is 180 kilometres from Berchtesgaden and is serviced by most major airlines from around the World. If no direct flight is available to Munich, then it is possible to connect through many airports such as Paris, Amsterdam and Frankfurt. On arrival at the airport you can either take the S-Bahn to the Hauptbahnhof (train station) to transfer to the train to Berchtesgaden or hire a car. Salzburg airport is closer, although it is serviced by fewer airlines. From the airport you can either hire a car, take the train, bus or a taxi.

Salzburg's W.A. Mozart airport is the second largest in Austria. You can fly direct to Salzburg with either major carriers or low cost airlines from many European cities including Berlin, Düsseldorf, Amsterdam, Vienna, Paris, London and Manchester. Alternatively you can connect via Frankfurt, Vienna, London and Amsterdam. The airport has recently been extended with the building of the Amadeus Terminal 2 to help cope with the increasing number of passengers and flights. You will find more flights available between November and March for skiing. The airport is only a 15-minute shuttle bus or taxi ride from the city centre.
www.salzburg-airport.com

## Useful Information

**Tourist Information**
Visitors Centre
Königsseer Strasse 2
83471 Berchtesgaden
Monday to Friday 8am to 5pm
(Opposite train station)

Mozartplatz 5
5020 Salzburg
9am – 6pm Monday to Saturday
www.salzburg.info/de

Salzburg Airport
Innsbrucker Bundesstrasse 95
(No times available)

Salzburg Railway Station
Bahnsteig 2a
9am – 6pm Monday to Sunday

**Emergency Numbers**
Police			110
Fire / Medical		112

**British Consulate**
Alter Markt 4
5020 Salzburg
0043 662 848133
9.30 – Midday Tuesday to Thursday

**US Consulate General**
51 Giselakai
5020 Salzburg
0043 662 28601

**Public Holidays in Salzburg and Bavaria**
On these days you will find most restaurants will be open, but all the shops and some attractions may be closed.

New Year's Day (1st January)
Epiphany (6th January)
Good Friday / Karfreitag
Easter Monday
May Day (1st May)
Ascension
Whit Monday
Corpus Christi
Annunciation (15th August)
Day of German Unity (3rd October)
All Saints (1st November)
Christmas Day and Boxing Day

# About The Author

Yvonne Salisbury was born in Newcastle upon Tyne, England, is married to Stephen and has two daughters. Yvonne has been visiting Germany for over 30 years but it is to Bavaria and in particular Munich that her heart belongs. She has been visiting this beautiful area with friends and family, several times a year for more than 20 years.

In recent years Yvonne has created her own websites for the area and also written several guides as well as freelance articles for The Daily Telegraph and The Munich Times. She was voted Simonseeks "Writer of the Month" for November 2009 and is a travel expert on Munich and the Oktoberfest. "My guides differ from others," says Yvonne "I have been and actually experienced what I write about, I started as a visitor myself and therefore believe I understand what the visitor needs to know".

"I have visited the Oktoberfest for over 20 years. It's so big, it's impossible to see it all in a single visit", says Yvonne Salisbury. "My Oktoberfest guide is ideal for first timers and lederhosen-veterans alike. Visit my site before you go, not to miss the best!"

**Websites by Yvonne Salisbury**, including details of how to buy guides

www.insidersguide-online.com

## Also by Yvonne Salisbury

**Beer, Bratwurst and Breze**
All of the detailed information you need is here about restaurants, shopping, and sightseeing. This is a must have volume for anyone really wanting to make the most of their Munich holiday.

Originally 3 guide books written by herself about Munich, Oktoberfest, Beer Gardens and their culture and the Christmas Markets, Yvonne has combined them all into this one handy book "Beer, Bratwurst and Breze". It includes details of many attractions for you to see, daytrips, walking tours, details of festivals throughout the year including Oktoberfest and the Christmas Markets, over 50 recommended restaurants and beer gardens and places to eat, many insider "top tips" and more than 100 photographs. The author visits Munich several times a year for over 25 years so she knows this subject well. All information has been gathered personally, not found on Wikipedia and such like, that's what makes our Insiders' Guides unique.

http://blog.insidersmunich.com/
https://twitter.com/InsidersMunich

**Brandenburg, Beer and Brunch**
Your guide to a city break in Berlin, a vast, fascinating city and a monument of living history, where East meets West and old meets new. Berlin is not stifled by its past, it is pushing forward with shiny new developments and trendy bars to attract the young crowd. There is plenty to see; historians will enjoy the remnants of the wall, Hitler's Bunker and the new Jewish Synagogue Centre; culture lovers will enjoy the many museums, galleries and theatres and if that is not for you then there is shopping, palaces, sports, festivals and great outdoor spaces. Families are not forgotten with children's museums, play parks and activities. Berlin has something to offer everyone; here every one can find their own Berlin. Brandenburg, Beer and Brunch includes details of over 45 attractions for you to see as well as a 7 flexible tours, details of festivals throughout the year including an overview of the Christmas Markets, over 25 recommended restaurants and places to eat, "off the beaten track" tips for each district plus insider "top tips" and colour photographs.

All available from www.insidersguide-online.com and Amazon.com

Printed in Great Britain
by Amazon